A Dwelling Place for Wisdom

A Dwelling Place for Wisdom

Raimon Panikkar

Translated by Annemarie S. Kidder

Westminster/John Knox Press
Louisville, Kentucky

The major portion of this text was originally published in German as *Der Weisheit eine Wohnung Bereiten* (Munich: Kösel Verlag, 1991).

Book design by Laura Lee

First edition

This book is printed on acid-free paper that meets the American National Standards Institute Z39.48 standard. ⊗

Published by Westminster/John Knox Press
Louisville, Kentucky

PRINTED IN THE UNITED STATES OF AMERICA

9 8 7 6 5 4 3 2 1

Library of Congress Cataloging-in-Publication Data
Panikkar, Raimundo
   [Weisheit eine Wohnung bereiten. English]
   A dwelling place for wisdom / Raimon Panikkar ; translated by Annemarie S. Kidder. — 1st ed.
       p.   cm.
   Includes bibliographical references and index.
   ISBN 0-664-25362-8 (pbk. : alk. paper)

   1. Life. 2. Wisdom. 3. Religions. 4. Philosophy, Comparative. 5. Tradition (Philosophy) 6. Self (Philosophy) 7. Christianity and other religions—Hinduism. 8. Hinduism—Relations—Christianity.
I. Title.
BD435.P2613   1993
128—dc20   92-19450

Contents

Contents

Preface

Gaudens gaudebo in Vita, quia in corde hominis
iucundam sibi Sapientia mansionem paravit.

I shall rejoice in Life because Wisdom has prepared
a glorious dwelling place for itself in the human heart.

Wisdom is the art of life. This could be a simple description of a basic human experience, expressed by peoples in almost all cultures in various ways and called by different names. Wisdom is a *savoir vivre*, whereby *savoir* does not mean knowledge *about* life, but simply intellectual experience *of* life.

No one can live without wisdom. The wise sustain the world, according to almost all religions. But the modern world would hardly admit to that and, as a result, is obsessed with the need for security. Wisdom has been taken out of life's traffic into a nursing home, where it stays locked up (sometimes even under tender care). Even broadmindedness can be a business.

According to many traditions, wisdom is a fine lady, even a queen, who presents herself in a mysterious triad that makes for the fullness of human life: an objective attitude, true insight, and proper action. Christian scholars would say *esse–scire–posse,* or *unitas–veritas–bonitas,* or something like that. Indian tradition speaks of *karma–bhakti–jñāna,* or *artha–kāma–dharma,* or even *sat–cit–ānanda.* The Jainas speak of thinking, speaking, and acting; the Chinese of Man, the Heavens, and the Earth.

Experts in both East and West have claimed this lady, named wisdom, as their own. Be they theologians, brahmins, philosophers, mandarins, priests, or doctors—all have claimed to rule over wisdom and to have access to a special entry gate to wisdom's dwelling place. Once in a while these groups have condescended to inform the common people what wisdom had told, even revealed, to them. At times these groups have prescribed what science was to examine and what its teachings had to be. Although the imprisoned fine lady was celebrated as the queen of science, she was in a tighter spot than any constitutional queen. She could only put her signature on what was presented to her.

Noble figures such as Socrates, Buddha, Lao-tzu, and Jesus tried to liberate wisdom and to provide access to it; however, chief inquisitors of all kinds thought they knew better how to deal with the masses. Yet these eminent figures exercise an inexplicable magnetism and have for thousands of years. They may no longer have power, but they still have an undiminished authority. The sage is not a professional, such as a king, a priest, or a scientist; the sage has no power, such as of the state, God, or science; the sage's authority, which could turn him or her into an advisor, has a much different origin.

I could have situated these reflections on wisdom in the history of thought, but then the rather existential character of this book might have been lost. My interpretation tries in general to avoid theological and cosmological controversies, because this is not a purely academic work. Becoming familiar with wisdom is more than theoretical reflection on it.

The subject of this book is the wisdom of life. In most religions the idea of "wisdom as the seat of freedom" is well known. Wisdom provides us with happiness and joy. It is the dwelling place where we can be at home, where we can be ourselves; and that means blessed. The characteristic of wisdom is joy, *ānanda, charis, beatitudo,* blessedness. This deep and unperturbable joy is an immediate fruit of wisdom. Wisdom leads to joy, and we are responsible for our joy. Although the bodhisattva has abandoned his *nirvāna,* he is not a sad creature but is full of joy. This fact cannot be explained by reason alone. There is suffering in the world which concerns me and is my suffering also; yet I am not overcome by sadness. Why joy and sorrow can harmonize cannot be explained rationally.

Why are we responsible for our joy? One metaphysical anthropology has a simple answer: The goal of human nature, of any nature, is blessedness. If we do not reach this goal, it is a sign that we are headed in the wrong direction.

The kingdom of wisdom, paradoxically, can be entered by all because it transcends both sensuousness and intelligibility and takes its seat in the mystical. To use the language of Indic cultures, primarily buddhist, we might say that the kingdom of wisdom (*jñāna*) is already present where morality (*shila*) and peaceful insight of the soul (*dhyāna*) have been reached: wisdom penetrates both morality and insight.

Wisdom has always been the wealth of the common people. Even today, wherever wisdom finds an outlet, it is present in the sayings, parables, and narratives of the various peoples, be it in Africa, Asia, or elsewhere. Wisdom resides in the spoken rather than in the written word. Wisdom books are, by and large, collections of oral tradition that have been intensified and refined by the sieve of time.

This book originates from the spoken word as well. Writing it would have been impossible for me without the efforts of three friends. Irmgard Hafner invited me to give a lecture, whose title she formulated herself and is the title of this book. Bogdan Snela invited me to lead a retreat and took on the responsibility of engineering it all into a book. Christoph Bochinger had the difficult task of editing my style and transforming my notes into a cohesive presentation.

The third and fourth parts of this book, translated by him from english into german, originated likewise with the invitations of three good friends: Paolo Soleri, famous architect and prophet from Arcosanti, Arizona, U.S.A., wanted a "personal statement" for his conference "Minds for History"; André Mercier, renowned professor of physics at the University of Berne, Switzerland, and also philosopher, wanted a description of my philosophy for the series *Philosophische Selbstbetrachtungen* by the Fédération Internationale des Sociétés de Philosophie; and friends at the Claremont Graduate School in Claremont, California, U.S.A., held a meeting of theologians for exploring the problem of christology at the present, which later resulted in a book.

To all these I feel obliged and want to express my gratitude. I also want to thank my attentive audiences and, especially, those who did ask me questions. All have prompted me to say something of possible value. Without them much would have remained unexpressed and hidden in the dark.

Note concerning language: Modern languages are marked by the patriarchalism of both the past and the present. It is high time to overcome the latter, and our time is in desperate need of helping the feminine dimension of life and women, in particular, to regain their rights. But neither a matriarchalism (as much as we might long for it at times) nor a dualism between males and females is a satisfactory solution.

The Latin word for Man is *homo;* it signifies neither male nor female but the totality of Man where there are polarities but no divisions. Sex, gender, and polarity—the biological gender, the grammatical gender, and the polar structure of reality—are three different things. Feminine and masculine are not the same as woman and man. Even though the gender of the german words "sun" and "nose" is feminine and "river" and "stomach" are masculine, these things are not, biologically speaking, either feminine or masculine. *Yin* and *yang,* warm and cold, light and darkness are polarities that belong to reality as a whole and cannot be reduced to either "male" or "female" since the biological gender is just one of many polarities. I would call this reduction sexomorphism, or the sexomorphization of reality—our modern urge to squeeze all diversity into the paradigm of one differentiation, viewing reality only in the image of the human being (anthropomorphous) and the human being only in the image of gender (sexomorphous). The grammatical gender of the german word *Mensch* (Man) is masculine: "He" means gender, not sex. For decades I have been pleading for a new gender, not for the neuter (neither/nor, hence castration) but for the *utrum* (both/and, hence in all of reality, and therefore also in areas of thinking about the divine, the human, and the cosmic). Meanwhile, I use the masculine and regard it as inclusive without wanting to give the masculine the say over the whole and without wanting to proliferate fragmentation by means of repetitions (he-person/she-person, god/goddess, he-rock/she-rock, etc.) or by using the plural form. In sum, Man (not man) stands for *Mensch* and his uniqueness. I am not happy with equating Man and human or human being, even though I have used these here and there.

The fact that I am at home in several languages yet cannot command one in particular (because none is solely mine) makes me concentrate on the listening (and hence obeying) task in spoken language. For that reason, I pay close attention to the etymology of words and their relations, and I am convinced of the impossibility of a singular universal language. That is why I cite in this book foreign sayings in the original—something for which I want to thank my publisher greatly. These foreign sayings are simply to teach us that neither are we alone in our undertaking nor can we reduce every- thing to a single expression or language. Language—much like wisdom—has many dwelling places.

Kodaikkanal, December 8, 1990, Feast of Maria-Sophia
Tavertet, February 2, 1991, Feast of Lights

I. Preparing a Dwelling Place for Wisdom

Sapientia aedificavit sibi domum.

Wisdom has prepared a dwelling place for itself.
Proverbs IX:1

Since the 1930s the theme of this book has been a mantra to me, a music of words, which has accompanied me and with whose rhythm I have tried to live. Not only music can resound in us but also thoughts. The ear is not the only part that hears; the mind also does, and the whole body, all of one's being. The language of wisdom is able to unite the ear, the body, and the mind.

We are accustomed to reading words. We have almost stopped "eating" words, and we are even less used to letting words become flesh and embodying them. That is so even though both similes originate in the christian Holy Scriptures.

Preparing a dwelling place for wisdom—it is an invitation to build a happy home in the heart of Man. How can we incarnate these words? I would like to contribute to the practice of true spirituality with some reflections on wisdom. In the above phrase are contained three basic insights on human existence. We shall reflect on this phrase and perceive its meaning in the here and now without any rush, preconceived notions, or expectations.

Wisdom

1. All human traditions have praised wisdom in various forms and words and with varying emphases. Philosophy is one of the forms. Wisdom's ideal seems to be a human invariant. Every person and every people fathom and try to reach for something that can be called wisdom. But the notion of wisdom today is somewhat distorted in contrast to its traditional forms. Wisdom has always been easily forgotten; however, it has received a bad reputation these days,

having become distorted through the technocracy of this age and replaced by the great success of the scientific worldview. Wisdom has been displaced by what we call modern life. Today's life-style provides us with a plethora of information as well as with many conveniences. Modern wisdom appears as a rich, beautiful, educated lady, who doles out gifts, accommodates us in a comfortable and hospitable fashion, relays information, and makes us rich. The price of such advantages is the complication of our existence.

Nevertheless, this is not the traditional face of the lady. We have to rediscover, unveil, and look at this lady anew. We are no longer familiar with the true appearance of wisdom; it is hidden under the veil of wisdom's cosmetic beauty (see Job XXVIII:21). Whether scientists, business people, politicians, or even experts on religion—few of them are any longer striving to be sages. Instead, they equate wisdom with a kind of practical prudence, if with anything.[1] "I, wisdom, dwell with prudence" (Prov. VIII:12), wisdom says, but I am not identical with the latter. Wisdom demands insight, skill, and intelligence; however, wisdom supersedes all these—one should perhaps say, it "goes through and beyond them"—and then arrives at a different level of reality, another depth.

Those at home in the biblical tradition are familiar with the wisdom books and the wisdom-related statements of jewish tradition.[2] These old texts, commenting on circumstances relating to Egypt, tell what wisdom is like in a clearer fashion than I can describe here. I do not need to repeat these texts; instead I invite the reader to a personal reflection. I presuppose here a certain familiarity with this kind of wisdom literature; however, my intention is not to present a treatise about the past but a presentation by which we may experience wisdom.[3] I would like to play a little with wisdom, because I know it likes to be played with (Prov. VIII:30–31).

The word wisdom is etymologically related to *vidyā, veda, idein, videre,* vision, knowledge. The greek word *sophia* and the latin word *sapientia* point to experience, skillfulness, and taste. Although the word wisdom points to different contexts in other languages, the last two aspects seem to be always contained. St. Bonaventure clarifies that by deducing *sapientia* from *sapor* and *sapere,* from taste and knowledge (*Sententiarum* II,d.4, dub.2). Thereby he attests to an affective, sense-related, taste-related side and to an intellectual, cognitive, scientific side of wisdom. Wisdom is both *technê* and *epistêmê,* action and knowledge, practice and theory. "Wisdom is piety," the Bible says, Augustine comments, and Bonaventure repeats. It means that wisdom has a childlike, filial relationship to the source of all being.[4]

Heraclitus has said that *sôphronein,* healthy thinking, is the greatest virtue; wisdom, *sophia,* consists of speaking that which is true and of acting according to nature while listening to the latter.[5] "Only one thing is wise," he says in a different place, namely, "to recognize the insight which directs everything through everything."[6] This statement reminds of the *pratītyasamutpāda,* the "basic interrelatedness of all things" in buddhism,[7] as well as the *sarvam sarvātmakam,* the "all-in-all connection" in shivaism.[8]

Our first step, therefore, leads us to the insight that wisdom resembles a kind of integrated experience that shapes our life.

2. Rather than describing in further detail the various aspects of wisdom, we shall now focus on what is "unwise" and learn by its opposite what wisdom demands of us today. The opposite of wisdom is not clumsiness and ignorance, since wisdom has its place not only in action and knowledge. Further, the opposite of wisdom is not foolishness. Many times it is the fool or the idiot who is the sage, even in western literature. Etymology makes it clear that dumb (foolish) and dumb (mute) are interrelated, as are the respective german words *dumm* and *stumm.* According to the words' stems, foolishness is related to stammering, stuttering, hitting, and pushing. Often the sage is silent. It is enlightening and important for our time to hear what Heraclitus formulated in the best spirit of the western tradition. The opposite of wisdom is knowing it all, *polymathia.* To be precise, the *fountain* of knowing-it-all is true "nonwisdom." This fountain is a result of the urge to know many things. This urge, in turn—Buddha would add—is the source of all suffering. But if it exists in the person, one should not repress it in any way. Still, knowing-it-all does not, according to Heraclitus, produce understanding or procure wisdom.[9]

Heraclitus's remark had a polemic character already in its own time, during the fifth century B.C. Heraclitus had directed it at Xenophanes, and even at Pythagoras. The remark criticized instances where the method of specialization was used to gain wisdom. This basic polemic is all the more radical in light of philosophy's modern development. In what might be called a proleptic vision directed at Descartes, Heraclitus emphasized that genuine wisdom was impossible wherever knowledge has to be compartmentalized in order to know something about the world and its constituent parts. Heraclitus spoke out against the fragmentation of knowledge, against analysis as a necessary means for understanding.[10] That makes him highly relevant for today.

It is almost perverse how we are bombarded by information as if we needed the latter for living life as humans. Whatever we call scientific progress is nothing other than the expansion of specialized sciences that divide themselves more and more in order to enlighten us less and less. The real problem, however, is that this method has become a serious requirement for us and we now regard its analytical path as "natural." We say research, but we mean intervention in nature.

Whatever modern science may be, and whatever its advantages for the elite groups, the kind of knowledge that can be chopped to pieces, whose development forces a continued chopping process once one has started that way, is not wisdom at all. We find ever more subdivisions, make more discoveries, and come to more interesting and attractive results. In the end, however, we are unable to put things together—like a child who has taken apart a toy. We are no longer able to play because we are too occupied by the analysis of the various parts into which we have dissected reality.

The holistic attitude has been lost because the person has been reduced to reason, reason to intellect, and intellect to the ability to classify and to formulate laws about how things work. This kind of knowledge no doubt has its place in life and is even useful. The problem is not knowledge itself but our urge to take this analytical direction, thus forgetting the totality of things. We call it the oblivion of the self, the *ātman,* the forgetfulness of the whole whose center goes through us. (In order to avoid entanglement in philosophical discussions at this point, I do not mention the oblivion of being; though I assume that Heidegger has seen this problem too.)

Simplicity of wisdom is not an artificial simplification of life but the discovery that I am touching all of reality. It also means that I can approach and conceive of reality, if I do not forget myself, if I do not disconnect myself in the process, and if I do not objectify reality, thereby turning myself into a severed subject. An integrated experience takes place only when theory and practice meet, when my need for knowledge is not independent of my existence. It takes place whenever my heart preserves its purity. Many traditions say that seeking knowledge, the knowledge of good and evil, was the original sin of humankind (Gen. II:17). Sin means here the rejection of, and separation from, the interconnectedness of all being.

Thus, the second step of this reflection takes us closer to ourselves. It shows us that wisdom is, as a unifying approach to life, dependent on the transparency of our selves and the genuineness of our lives. Wisdom is personal harmony with reality, unity with existence, Tao, heaven, God, nothingness. . . .

3. Neither wisdom nor truth is exclusively a basic intellectual value. As already indicated, wisdom is an attitude stemming from experience and, therefore, presupposing both understanding and action, *sapere* and *sapor*. Not even the knowledge of wisdom is a merely rational action but, moreover, a touching of reality, a realization, which compares with a not-knowing. Both eastern and western traditions remind us of this fact continually. The occidental tradition of apophatism, of "enlightened not-knowing" (*docta ignorantia*) or the "cloud of unknowing," is more than two and a half thousand years old. "The person who is truly in connection with God in this life, is united to God as totally unknown" (*unitur ei sicut omnino ignoto*), Dionysius Areopagita says.[11] Thomas of Aquinas has confirmed this statement explicitly.[12] Aquinas is convinced that ultimate human knowledge of God lies primarily in knowing that we do not know God as God.[13] And Evagrius Ponticus exclaimed: "Blessed is he who has reached an infinite ignorance" (*agnôsia*).[14]

The wisdom of the *upanishads* tells us that we should strive not for multiplicity but for that by which, when discovered, we can understand everything.[15] Is there such a thing? Whereby could I understand that which causes all understanding to occur, which allows for understanding everything? Many traditions (if not almost all) have emphasized the active and transforming character of understanding: one becomes what one understands—at the same time understanding only that which one is ready to become. Medieval scholastics said it this way: one understands only what one loves. Most important is the kind of becoming that creates communion with reality.

Since not only truth but also wisdom has an existential character, both wisdom and truth belong together.[16] The *Rāmāyana* says: "In fact, the old sages and the Gods respected the truth (*satyam*): Whosoever speaks the truth in this world, enters the highest of dwelling places" (II,109,11). Another passage reads: "Wisdom (*satyam*) is God in the world. It is on wisdom that justice always is built. It is in wisdom that everything is rooted. There is no higher level above that" (II,109,13). "On wisdom (*satyam*) the earth rests, because of wisdom the sun shines, due to wisdom the wind blows: Everything depends on wisdom" (*Vriddha-Kānakja* V,19).[17] A passage of the *Mahābhārata* puts it this way: "Through wisdom the law (*dharma*) is preserved; through diligence and practice knowledge (*vidyā*) is preserved; through cleanliness beauty is preserved" (V,1132). Christian scholasticism states quite plainly that one "should set out by intellect and arrive at wisdom."[18] Truth leads to wisdom, but not automatically or by itself.

The human longing for wisdom is found everywhere, and it seems to be the most specific human longing. Plants love the light; animals want to be happy; human beings want happiness too, but only in a much deeper and intense fashion. Man is Man because he or she is able to gain wisdom and longs for it. The third eye, salvation, enlightenment, *satori,* the resurrection—all are symbols of wisdom. We can truly say that, in this sense, wisdom is a human invariant.

Wisdom is attained not by *knowing many things* but by *not knowing.* One has to go right through the intellect, thus not negating but transcending it. Only then is knowledge not an obstacle to living. The *Kena-Upanishad* tells us very harshly: "It is not understood by those who know it; it is understood by those who do not know it" (II,3).[19] This statement goes even beyond what Socrates said. It tells us that those who know do not understand. Hence, those who know that they do not know are still on the knowing side and do not really understand. Paul would call them "the sages of this world." They are the academicians, the professors, and all other self-declared "sages" who know that they do not know. But if they know that they do not know, they cannot be happy. Only those are sages who are so not-knowing that they are not even aware of this fact. There is absolutely no room for pretense here.

This statement is not a paradox but a deep human experience that can be felt by anyone. It is the total negation of any elitist concept concerning wisdom. Accordingly, the hebrew Bible states that anyone is allowed to go to wisdom and get strengthened by its fruits (Prov. IX:3ff.; Sirach XXIV:19).

Paul, however, introduced a dichotomy in the thought of christianity that contrasts with many other traditions in the history of religions. Paul speaks of two kinds of wisdom: the *sophia* of the world or of the flesh, and the *sophia* of God, the divine wisdom that will forever remain a mystery.[20] Paul's distinction resulted in a dualism in christian tradition from which many christians have not yet completely recovered. If this distinction was realistic and beneficial in Paul's situation, it gave rise to a special development in religious history whereby the basic traits of wisdom became obscured by time—with far-reaching consequences.

Our third step seems to leave us without a firm grasp on wisdom. "Those who know, do not talk; and those who talk, do not know" (*Tao-te king,* 56; cf. also 81). Whoever presumes to have "arrived," should be careful not to stumble, Paul warns. The street robber, the sinner, the slave . . . will be saved in the end, while the monk, the ascetic, the (apparent) saint will be lost, according to legends from all over the world. It is not the person who wills but the one who is "chosen," according to the *upanishads,* shivaism, and christianity. Hence, this third step leads us to pure grace, against which our will remains powerless.

A Dwelling Place

1. A dwelling place is not a garment. It is not an individual affair, not a kind of private salvation. It is not *for me.* I cannot simply occupy, manipulate, and enjoy wisdom. I cannot simply use it, not even for some beneficial cause; nor can I use it up or abuse it. Intellect, on the other hand, can be manipulated and used as a weapon. One can wrestle with intellect and win; one can overpower and persuade the less informed. The same is true for reason.[21] But it would be contrary to wisdom's nature to use it as a weapon, as a tool for a specific purpose. Wisdom is not an object. It is not even useful. It is good for nothing. It is not a servant. It is completely superfluous. It exists only where there is abundance, only where wisdom is

allowed to overflow out of its plentitude. One cannot adorn oneself with wisdom; one cannot attain wisdom; one cannot conquer, capture, and comprehend wisdom and then perhaps use it for a good cause. In short, no sort of individualism will ever locate wisdom.

The term "dwelling place," *oikos* in the Septuagint, does not at all mean what one might take it for nowadays: a more or less comfortable shelter, which "defends" us—etymologically speaking—and which contains all necessary amenities for our well-being so that our lives will be comfortable and, to a certain degree, joyful. "Building a dwelling place for wisdom" does not mean to furnish wisdom with a shelter to live in. It is a sign of this modern culture, obsessed with numbers, that in almost all cities, houses (and also streets) have lost their names or never had them in the first place; instead, houses are distinguished by numbers. "Building a dwelling place" does not mean overcoming some kind of homelessness the moment I know I have private property for which I own seven keys, and where I can enjoy the dividends of "wisdom." The oft-decried homelessness of the modern person results from the fact that scientific cosmology is not able to offer the person a human dwelling place. The scientific world is no dwelling place. The person is lost in the quantitative desert of an "expanding" universe and the chain of millions of years reaching back to our animal ancestors. The person is homeless because the scientific worldview has lost the human dimension, and even more so because this worldview's dwelling place has not been erected by wisdom but by an extrapolating calculation. In such a universe, it is impossible for the person to feel at home. Little wonder that mobility has become a characteristic of modern society. Millions of tourists are only roaming about, taking tours; U.S. citizens change their addresses once every four years on average. A home that has not been built by wisdom is not a home.

Hence, the first dimension of a dwelling place is the world as our homeland. The world is a dwelling place for all—for the homeless, the poor, the people. Bonaventure speaks, in true franciscan manner, of wisdom as multifaceted so that it can be experienced in many ways and become nebulous to the proud and plain to the lowly.[22] Wisdom is not complicated; it is not the sum total of many facets of knowledge, not even of multitudinous experiences. One cannot pile up and accumulate wisdom. There can never be a capitalization of wisdom. Rather, the dwelling place is a caravansary, an inn for caravans, with courts under open sky for each pilgrim in this world. May I interpret Meister Eckhart's "seclusion" (*Abgescheidenheit*) as an exclusion from every kind of exclusivism?[23]

Man resides in an inhabited and habitable world. One cannot experience wisdom unless one regards the whole world as one's own homeland. This is more difficult for modern Man though at times less dangerous than for former generations, since the average modern Man lives in a world devoid of angels, ghosts, Gods, winds, and other such beings. The city dweller does not live with animals in forests. Hence, we are unable to experience the world as a dwelling place by regarding ourselves solely as isolated atoms in a quantitative universe. We can no longer experience what astrology taught and Gregory the Great once proudly commented on: "Man is not made for the stars, but the stars for Man."[24] Thomas Aquinas enforces this view: "The wise person rules even over the stars."[25] Thus, both men acknowledge the premise of astrology, namely, that the person is connected with the stars. They only reject the subjection of the person to the stars' constellations.

In a word, the primary dwelling place of wisdom is our universe, our world, and still more concrete, our Mother Earth. In this way, I understand the word "ecosophy," which is to be distinguished from the word "ecology." Here is not the place to criticize the urge of this culture to leave this planet, an urge modern technology allows us to imagine as a certain possibility. One might interpret it as a *fuga mundi* (flight from the world); however, such a trip would not be a departure from earth but an escape from self. This syndrome contains a basic idea that is relevant to our topic: If one does not feel comfortable on Earth, if Earth is not a dwelling place for wisdom, then it is not surprising to dream of interstellar travels and to imagine leaving Earth. Then Earth is only some sort of blanket on which we "gravitate" because of Newton's law of gravity or on which we "sit"; it is something to which we have no inner relationship. The shaman is concerned with something totally different when leaving the physical body in order to commence the trip to heaven. The shaman leaves Earth with the purpose of returning to it and of bringing back something of the hidden wisdom for helping others. Such a trip is not an escape from Earth, because Earth is still the dwelling place.

Modern space trips, on the other hand, are an anthropological alienation, not to be compared with the urge of the Argonauts.

2. Dwelling place also means house; it is a building to be constructed. Proverbs IX:1 does not speak of a "habitat." It talks about the activity of building a temple, a house, a dwelling place—*oikodomeô, aedificare; oikia, aedes*. One might translate it as "to make a dwelling place livable," to furnish it as a dwelling place by means of moving into it. An uninhabitable or an actually uninhabited dwelling is no dwelling place at all—just as an unsung song is no song. But we are concerned here not with the meta-political aspect of the activity of dwelling but with the political aspect. (Politics means here the public activity of the person [*politeuma*], the human activity in the *polis,* and not the special occupation of the politician.)

Our text calls it a "dwelling place," not a cave or a ditch—and certainly not hell, a hidden place, or an esoteric mystery. The real mystery is open and accessible. True wisdom is simple and therefore perhaps hard to locate, but it certainly is not elitist.[26] "Nothing is hidden, except in order to shine forth" (Mark IV:22). Truly esoteric teaching is not another doctrine, but the invisible side of exoteric teaching; it remains invisible to those who have eyes but cannot see (see Isa. VI:9ff.; Matt. XIII:13; Mark IV:22ff.; John XII:40; etc.). "The big secret is that there is no secret," a "mysterious" text of shivaism from Kashmir says.[27] "The secrets of the heart which the person wants to hide, become conspicuous to all," the *Chung Jung* says (I,1,3).

Christianity's greatest reformulation of jewish sources lies in describing wisdom no longer as a privilege of the scholars, the aristocrats, the chosen ones, "the pious," the just—not even the "sages." Salvation is for all, and wisdom can be attained by prostitutes, samaritan women, tax collectors, the uncircumcised, and primarily the common, poor people, the *anawim* (cf. Matt. XI:25, for example). This fact may explain why Paul introduced a double meaning of wisdom.[28] Wisdom has a visible dwelling place: "One does not light a lamp and put it under a pitcher but on top of the lampstand; thus, it gives light to everyone in the house" (Matt. V:15; cf. Mark IV:21; Luke VIII:16; XI:23). A dwelling place is neither a cave for the "perfect" nor a castle for the privileged; it is a home for all (cf. John

XIV:2).[29] According to Bonaventure, "Our soul can be inhabited by divine wisdom as if it were a temple."[30] He adds that wisdom thereby becomes "the daughter of God, God's bride, and God's girl friend."

Therefore, a dwelling place is not only the earth, not this secret refuge as we still might say, but a house, a true homestead. It is a place to stay where we can settle down, a home where we can be ourselves, where we can have a human relationship with things. We do not need to hide this wisdom; neither do we have to protect or defend it. Just as a free person manages daily affairs without weapons, a true dwelling place in a truly human culture does not need electronic or other defense systems. True wisdom does not need a bodyguard, nor even a copyright. When invited to an armed home, wisdom flees immediately.

3. Sacred writings tell us that wisdom has a double dwelling place. On the one hand, it is the human heart (Hebrew *leb*) that is a dwelling place of wisdom (Prov. II:1); here heart symbolizes the totality of the person.[31] The heart is understood in an intellectual, spiritual, and physical sense; it follows the rhythm of nature, being at the same time in contact and symbiosis with other hearts. On the other hand, it is the entire earth that is a dwelling place of wisdom (Prov. VIII:22–31). Hence, a dwelling place is neither just a small house nor a certain community or civilization but the human heart and the earth at large. "In the good heart of Man (lies) wisdom," the Bible says (Prov. XIV:33), and the Earth is its dwelling place (Prov. VIII:2ff.). The *Rig Veda* sings: "By carefully pondering within their hearts, the sages found the connection between being and non-being" (X,129,4). An *upanishad* says it even more precisely: "Truth (wisdom) is understood with the heart; because, certainly, truth (wisdom) makes its home (has its basis, roots) in the heart."[32]

The chinese, the indic, and the christian traditions speak of the heart of the world and discover a close correlation with the human heart: "Just as big as the universal space (*ākāsha*) is the space in the heart (*antar-hriday'ākāsha*). In the heart lie heaven and earth, fire and wind, sun and moon, lightnings and stars, what is (among us) and what is not (among us); everything is contained in it" (CU VIII,1,3).

Another *upanishad* repeats what later became a common conviction: "The heart is truly *brahman*. . . . The heart is its dwelling place

17

(*āyatana*—where one enters and remains), the space (*ākāsha*), its basis (*pratishthā*) which one has to recognize in order to be stable. . . . The heart is the dwelling place of all being, the basis of all being; all beings rely on the heart" (BU IV,1,7).

It is well known among semitic peoples that the heart (hebrew *leb;* akkadian *libba*) is also connected with *rûach* (the personal human spirit), *nefesh* (soul, life), *neshamah* (breath), kidneys, and flesh. The same seems to apply to african cultures. In a word, the heart is the center of the person and as such is the seat of wisdom. The center has the same distance from every point of the circle. The wise one is even-tempered, fair, and unbiased, chinese classical literature emphasizes. In sum, wisdom is not an area of specialization.

Wisdom without its dwelling place is not wisdom but simply an abstraction, a term. Wisdom has to be incarnate; it has to be rooted. There cannot be a dwelling place without foundations! Without personal experience, without wisdom's dwelling place, wisdom is nothing. Inhabiting and being are even etymologically connected. Inhabiting is the way of being to wisdom. One inhabits as one makes a sojourn, as one discovers a place. One does not simply live anywhere but in or at a certain *where*. This *where* is the Earth, the home, and the human heart. Wisdom is always only a guest. For good reason, hospitality was the first of people's duties toward their neighbors. One should receive wisdom as a mother would conceive a child. But we cannot give birth to wisdom on our own accord, just as that is not possible for a woman alone. Every conception needs a womb. The dwelling place is wisdom's womb. Wisdom lives in us in the same way that the incarnation is experienced by christian mystics: "And it lived among us" (John I:14)—yet often only pitching a tent (*eskênôsen*) because we do not open up our heart as a dwelling place for it.

Hugh of St. Victor in the western tradition of the twelfth century offers a short formula of what since Augustine was a common view. There are, he says, three houses: the whole world, human society, and the personal soul. All three are dwelling places of the divinity, the "houses of God." The divine, the human, and the cosmic, we could translate, have the same dwelling.[33] To prepare a dwelling place for wisdom amounts to being rooted in the hearth of reality.

Preparing

1. A dwelling place does not exist readily. It is not something that nature provides; it is something that culture provides. We have already said that one has to inhabit a dwelling place. An empty home is no home. A purely theoretical wisdom is no wisdom. Wisdom does not enter an uninhabited dwelling place. But before moving into a home, one has to—perhaps at the same time—construct, build, and furnish it: One has to prepare it.

Some biblical texts say that it is the woman who builds a dwelling place for wisdom (Prov. XIV:1). In similar fashion, indic texts say that the woman preserves the home, just as the *dharma* preserves well-being (riches).[34] Thus, building a home is not the job of engineers but rather resembles the process of giving birth. The *Atharva Veda* says that the home is formed by ritual and built by the sages (IX,3,19). How can one prepare a home?

One should never go out looking for wisdom. One can only begin by preparing a dwelling place for wisdom. The adage "Seek wisdom!" cannot mean that one should chase after wisdom as if it were an object, a thing one could hunt for. Wisdom is not the end of a long pilgrimage. According to the biblical passages, wisdom outdoes the pearls of beauty (see Prov. III:15; Wisd. of Sol. VII:29–30; Job XXVIII:18; and Prov. XXXI:10). When skipping to other traditions, one hears Chuang-tzu say that this miraculous pearl can only be found by means of unintentionality. Each kind of search would leave fingerprints on the pearl and take away its glamour, as if one were to touch the wings of a butterfly. One has to become surprised by the pearl's beauty, become transformed by it. No power of reasoning, no effort, no search leads to this end. The search for wisdom would stain wisdom's independence and soil its sovereign liberty. There are two possibilities: Either I want to be the ruler of wisdom and treat her as my servant, demanding this and that, wanting knowledge, power, and diversion, and, I may even be able to get those things—or, I allow myself to become penetrated, enlightened, and inhabited by wisdom. In the latter case, the initiative lies with wisdom, and that belongs to nature's proper order, so that everything I could find besides would no longer be true wisdom to me. "Whoever finds me, finds life" (Prov. VIII:35). Hence it is not wisdom that is to be found, but life; not some retrieved object, but one's own true life. Wisdom is not an object. One cannot set out searching for it.

It is appropriate that when standing before wisdom, we hold no power. After all, wisdom itself is without power. Wisdom only bestows authority, lending it to those who allow themselves to be visited by it spontaneously. Wisdom is neither an object of the intellect nor of the will. This statement was one of the main doctrines of the Buddha: Each kind of craving, even the desire for *nirvāna,* destroys both the one who searches and what is being searched. At this point, a linguistic differentiation between spontaneous aspiration (the "spiration," the very breath of the spirit: *Betrachtung;* cf. *tractare, trachten,* aspire) and conscious desire might be helpful.

We can illustrate what has been said through a chinese narrative (slightly altered) by Huang Po (*Hsi-yün*), a *Ch'an* master of the ninth century. This narrative tells of a lonely seeker standing at the foot of a mountain and crying out in intense and desperate ways—in order to find wisdom. Finally, he hears a voice from the top of the mountain, which seems to answer him. He hears it very clearly and so clambers up the mountain. Once he is there, everything is calm—no voice, no sound. Disappointed, he goes back down; he knows from books that one should not give up quickly, and so he starts crying out again— one could also say he prayed, explored, searched, applied himself. Then he hears the voice again, and again he climbs up the mountain. Nothing! It goes on like this for a while. When he eventually comes back down and gives up, the man hears nothing else. Then he discovers that what he heard had been nothing but the echo of his own voice.[35] Should I compare this story with that of Prometheus? Preparing means waiting.

2. Hence, preparing is not a pursuit after wisdom; still, it means being ready. Strictly speaking, we are not talking about a kind of preparation in view of what is to come. Wisdom cannot be manipulated, not even in expectation's subtle ways. Hope does not relate to the future; it relates to the invisible dimensions of reality and not to something yet to come.

Our text does not tell us that it is sufficient to be prepared for the arrival of wisdom, that wisdom will appear automatically as soon as we are ready. Instead it tells us that wisdom itself will prepare a dwelling place. We do not have to get involved in the process. Any kind of egocentric spirituality steered by our own will is suspicious. The preparation on our part consists of placing trust in wisdom, which means that we acquire confidence in reality, an attitude described by the classics as, for example, *rita, dharma, kosmos, taxis, ordo.*

Such preparedness requires purity of the heart, an idea that might be illustrated by the seclusiveness (*Abgeschiedenheit*) of the mystics of the Rhineland and the *shūnyatā* of the buddhist *Prajñāpāramitā* tradition. We should not use force on wisdom, not expect positive results from our deeds. That is what the *Bhagavadgītā* (III,4; IV,18–21; XVII,49) and other wisdom doctrines teach. The *Gītā* says—possibly in reference to buddhist teachings (cf. *Dīghanikāya*, III,275)—that the person is wise (*buddhimān*) when standing above her deeds. One does not prepare oneself for wisdom. One lives as one wants to, has to, should live; one lives as one does, regardless of merits and possible advantages based on one's deeds. One might mention here the beautiful zen narratives stating that the master eats when eating and sleeps when sleeping and does nothing else besides, or that for the enlightened one rivers are once again rivers, mountains are mountains, and the marketplace the marketplace.

Wisdom is free; it is a present, a pure gift. Our readiness for wisdom is an end in itself, not a means by which to acquire wisdom. The person can only be found by wisdom, not set out in search of it. Or, to be more precise: We only have to care about not putting any obstacles in the way. And, to be even more precise: We have to act as if we were leaving wisdom alone, letting wisdom be what she is meant to be—whether she comes looking for us or not. Is wisdom not meant to be free? Do we want to lock her up in the cage of expectations? It has become difficult for us, people of a patriarchal civilization, to take the middle road between passivity and activity. Did we not find out that the means that helped us gain self-control, acquire certain virtues, or reach a degree of perfection (to speak with the words of the old schools) could also become the biggest obstacles in our attempt to live life authentically? Being quite simply means *being;* leaving being as it is, not interrupting being by means of violence, activities, thoughts; leaving being's activities alone. It would be totally wrong to view such an attitude as quietism, even though the danger of a certain quietist rigidity might be present. But where there is life, there is danger.

We are talking here about the art of trusting, of experiencing, of observing, and of respecting being. When choosing to experiment with things, we end up using violence on them and become impatient. We become impatient because we are not in harmony with the rhythms of being and because these rhythms are not enough for us. They are not enough for us because we do not want to leave being alone, which means that we ourselves do not want to be. In this impatience, our longing for death becomes apparent—*thanatos,* death, pulling us to an unconscious death drive. Being is not static; it has its own inner rhythm, which needs to be discovered. *Preparing* means hoping.

3. But what can this kind of *preparing* look like? Preparing does not mean conquering, studying, or prearranging. It deals with the feminine attitude of preparedness, the art of good faith, of being quiet. Preparing means neither overpowering wisdom by searching for it nor preparing ourselves in the secret hope that wisdom might visit us. In order for wisdom to build a dwelling place for itself, it needs freedom. This freedom has a name, which has been bestowed by many wisdom traditions, although it has suffered from a bad reputation in some circles. The name is grace.

One cannot *dole out* grace. No one can distribute it; that would be unfair (here the distortion starts that finds expression in the power and might of God's executives and their idea of a monarchic God). Yet one can *receive* grace. This idea is foreign to us, since mere receiving does not match up with the servile attitude of the subordinated. Fear is not a virtue in this case. Only love allows us to receive, and it produces fruit from what has been received. We want to fight for peace, but we rarely are ready to simply receive it. We want to pay the price for every single item, for each measure, and we call that justice, but we are hardly able to accept something offered to us for free. We want to find a cause, even a reason, for everything; but we are hardly ready to receive something given out of mere grace. In one word, we want this and that, but we do not want to give up our will. Perhaps we no longer are able to do so. Our not wanting still equals a wanting. The kingdom of grace lies outside of all we want and do not want. Wisdom is pure grace.

Tao-te king XXV says:

> There is one thing, which is indiscriminately perfect. Even before the heavens and the Earth came into being, it was present. So calm, so alone. It stands by itself and never changes. It circles yet does not change position. One could call it: mother of the world. But I really do not know its name. I simply call it the *tao*. . . . The man finds orientation through the earth, the earth through the heavens, the heavens through the *tao,* the *tao* through itself.

We must stop somewhere in our reflections, and it is there that the kingdom of wisdom starts. The preparation of a dwelling place appears now almost as a vicious circle: If I want to construct a dwelling place, I will destroy it; if I do not want to, nothing will get done either. If I allow wisdom to prepare a dwelling place for itself, I will be somewhat aware that it will do so eventually and we will be dwelling together. How can I not wish for that? Yet because of such a wish, how can I avoid reducing wisdom to my own expectations, thus limiting its freedom? The art lies in transforming this *circulus vitiosus,* this short circuit, into a *circulus vitalis,* a living circle. Everything depends on the source, the reason for one's searching, the source of one's questioning, one's spontaneity in living. Jesus was asked, "Where do you live?" (John I:38). Those asking the question were most likely familiar with the questions of wisdom tradition: "But where does one locate wisdom?" "Where does wisdom come from?" "Where is her home?" "Where does she live?" (see Job XXVIII:12, 20). Yet the question the people asked Jesus was not a repetition of this; instead it already constituted an answer, namely, an embarrassed one. After all, Jesus had asked them: "What are you looking for?" But they did not know what they wanted. They had only been attracted by his radiating figure. Jesus' answer was not noetic (similar to the answer of the angel in Luke I:34–35). "Come and see," Jesus said (John I:39). Hence, both practice and experience matter; there are no quick recipes for wisdom.

But how can we build a dwelling place for this wisdom without being able to recognize it first, without knowing anything of it? I do not know ahead of time whether it is wisdom that is coming or a ghost, an impostor, a liar, a thief, an unwelcome guest. Our hospitality is genuine only when we do not know the guest ahead of time, when we do not select; it is not real when we only accept the sages, the believers, the members of our own social caste. But hospitality is real when we accept the guest, regardless of standing or appearance and without any form of discrimination. Not even Abraham knew for sure who was visiting him (Genesis XVIII)—three angels or three thieves, he could not tell. Hospitality with conditions attached is not hospitality but only a business—tourism, for example.

Such guests of old have been a king's daughter, an angel, the devil, a lion, Christ himself. All traditions tell us that when we invite the stranger, the unknown, the unsightly, and the unintelligible, the room where revelation can take place will form. This kind of hospitality is a form of surrender, a risk. It could get dangerous when opening up a dwelling place for everybody and everything without any criteria and differentiations. Here is where danger lurks. It is easy to say that we will prepare a dwelling place for wisdom, that we like accommodating wisdom and giving everything for it, that we like opening our hearts to wisdom so it can reform and transform us. But we do not know what wisdom looks like, what it is, and where it has lived before. This is the risk, the step in the open, freedom itself. Our "alchemic" activity here is to transform the guest who might not have been wisdom to begin with.

When we take this step, receiving becomes a genuine conceiving. Then preparing a dwelling place for wisdom means receiving the stranger, the unknown, that which plainly seems threatening; preparing means allowing the received to bud, blossom, develop, and be born. It is an activity for which the simile of biological childbirth is not even strong enough. It has to be a *theandric* activity. It is a wrestling with the guest, with what could be transformed into wisdom, with God, with the angel, with the You. All in all, it is about polarity at large—not about two individually developed characters that are opposed to each other but about a genuine polarity that has grown out of itself and from which everything else draws its existence. Wisdom is unknown until we, the I and the You, encounter each other. It is not wisdom until I have received it. It cannot be received by me and impregnate me as long as I am not wrestling with, absorbing, and somehow beginning an intimate interchange with it: In this polarity rests the transforming power of conceiving. This is the metamorphosis, the transformation of the vicious circle into a living circle, a *circulus vitalis*. It goes without saying that we cannot conceive a child by will power alone. Another person must be part of it—and love as well.

We have said earlier that there is no proof on our part and no identification card on the other. Everything remains open, and the possibility of a mistake is always present. Wrestling for wisdom is always open-minded and humble. There is, however, an internal experience by which we can recognize wisdom as such. Its name is peace, joy, and freedom. Hence, by its fruits we will recognize wisdom (cf. Matt. VII:16, 20). Wisdom also has an external characteristic. Thus, Chuang-tzu (IV,1) says of the sage: "He needs his inner eye, his inner ear in order to penetrate things and does not need reasoning of the intellect." And he continues: "Such a person is visited by those invisible, so they can *prepare a dwelling place in him;* how much more will he be visited by other people then. In this way, the world can be transformed" (following R. Wilhelm's translation).

Preparing a dwelling place for wisdom: We are talking here about a basic attitude, needed today more than ever. It means, in a negative sense, that we should not squander our time with all kinds of things—although they may be important and pleasant—which do not constitute wisdom, do not bring salvation, and do not allow for joy to appear. All of us have known about this truth for a long time. One does not need to add anything new, only to recall the old. After all, we know all about this truth, but we have no time for it.

An islamic legend recounts that when Allah saw and recognized the sad condition of the people, how they were treating the earth, he decided to once again send Archangel Gabriel back to Earth. In a way, he thought, the Koran is too difficult and too long, Gabriel will have to state it again in very simple terms. It will reverse the ecological catastrophe and make believers more straightforward, their faith more effective, and fundamentalism unnecessary. So Gabriel set out with this simple, plain wisdom message. He traveled everywhere, used all aides of the heavenly hosts and finally, after a long time, returned to heaven. His wings were totally soiled, and he was completely exhausted. Allah asked him how he, Gabriel, had fared, whether he had delivered the message. "Oh, sure," Gabriel said. "But people did not have time to listen!"

The solution is very simple, but we can find it only in quietude. . . .

Questions and Answers on Wisdom

You talked about the rhythm of being and about a subconscious death drive, supposedly responsible for our not being satisfied with this rhythm. This is a paradox. Why acceleration, if ultimately I am gravitating toward death?

Being is a verb, an action, and it has rhythm. I believe that the most important characteristic of technoscientific civilization lies in having introduced acceleration, less in the mathematical-physical than in the global sense: acceleration of rhythms, of times, of all happenings on this earth. Nowadays one thinks that the natural rhythms, the changes of day and night, of walking and sitting, of winter and summer—as in farming, for example—are no longer sufficient. One wants to progress faster. And the kind of acceleration resulting from this shatters the rhythms of the whole environment and of being in general. We are almost trying to speed up the process of life as a whole, thereby all the more speeding up the arrival of the parousia, the end of the world. Thus, we ourselves shorten life and force death to arrive all the sooner.

Being, however, has its own rhythm and it takes vengeance, so to speak, in light of such artificial restrictions. Rabindranath Tagore says: "How can you make the flower grow faster by pulling on its leaves?" The paradox here is the fact that one approaches death all the quicker the more one is afraid of death.

How does wisdom deal with power, the urge for domination?

Wisdom does so by not acknowledging the power of the powerful and by not allowing itself to feel threatened by power, even when life is at stake. That is not easy and will not always lead to immediate success. Moreover, it might not always be recommendable because there are real powers in this life. This Earth is a battlefield, and sometimes it is the fate of wisdom to be killed. Who knows . . . ! But when confronting one power with another power, nothing results apart from a mutual armament on all levels of life, in military aspects as well as in others. Yet if one is not afraid—this kind of fear cannot be controlled by mere will power—then the power of the powerful is voided. There is a childlike nature which cannot be artificially arranged and produced, and which as such has disarming effects.

The question possibly involves the realization that one should not always presuppose victory. One must limit the situation neither to the individual nor to the present viewpoints. The experience of the past eight thousand years of human history shows, if nothing else, that victories ultimately never lead to peace. Victory leads to victory, and one can forget about the defeated for a while. But perhaps after five hundred years, the defeated might get back on their feet—I am thinking here of the american continent. If we really want peace, we must not limit ourselves solely to attaining victory.

You are talking in a relatively skeptical way about the methods of analyzing, dissecting, experimenting, and all-comprehensive know-ing. But I am under the impression that you yourself know quite a lot. That is also apparent from your biographical data. Is there not, perhaps, a necessity to know a lot so one can restrain oneself by means of this amount of knowledge?

There certainly is always a way of retreating, a *retractatio*. But what I have said about the danger of knowing a lot, the so-called *polymathia*, does not mean that we should not, or must not, know anything. It means that we take this knowledge as a starting point and that we never sever it from the source of wisdom. There is an artificial innocence among people which makes them forget their responsibilities. This is nothing other than an escape from life and a cowardlike fear. It would be wrong to interpret our reflections as saying that we could do away with anything else in order to seek wisdom. It might be justified in some singular cases, but it cannot be true for all. Our pilgrimage is always a human pilgrimage. Since we live now in a society where specific and fragmented knowledge is necessary for survival, let us not ignore that. Yet at the same time, we should not forget two things:

1. *As little information as possible, and as thorough as possible.* We should try doing without unnecessary "knowledge." Nowadays, my whole life would not suffice in order to read and absorb all the

literature available on a particular "scientific" subject. Hence, we need to have a nose for it and develop criteria for choosing; we also need to allow ourselves to be advised by those who have an already greater understanding than we. Otherwise, I get sick when stepping into a library. After all, there lurks the temptation to find out about everything, and I must admit to myself that I cannot do that. One should always ask whether or not all these certain pieces of information constitute true knowledge.

2. *Not pulling out the root of wisdom.* We all have a sense for that. We sense when knowledge can enrich us, when it gives us more life, or when it confuses and derails us, leading us where we do not want to go, though we might allow it to do so anyway—perhaps because of desiring prestige or money. Resisting the temptation of this kind of instrumentality is as difficult as it is important.

How are "wisdom" and "truth" related?

When we mention the words "wisdom" and "truth" in the english language, our analytical way of thinking immediately differentiates. In sanskrit, however, one could use for both the single word *satyam,* "that which corresponds to being and originates from being." I have called it "beingness" (*Seiendheit*), "the sum total of all being in each being." It is true also for the greek language, where *sôphrosynê, alêtheia,* and *sophia* (intelligence, truth, and wisdom) are interrelated. According to the *Rāmāyana* or the *Mahābhārata,* for example, wisdom is absent from the one not living in the realm of truth and not speaking according to truth. Speaking the truth is possible only when one is living in the truth—and that is wisdom. The greek idea of wisdom does not mean that one should be unaware of life's dangers and simply allow these to attack; neither does it mean to perform a mental striptease in front of every question, not wanting to hold back anything. Wisdom is more than that, and it never has just one meaning. All living words are *polysemic;* that is, they have many nuances and connotations.

One cannot capture that in a system of coordinates or describe it with just a single voice. As a result, one needs to distinguish between the *term* wisdom and the *symbol* wisdom, the latter of which is the subject here. The kind of wisdom, for example, that is completely severed from intelligence, truth, and also justice, would be a nicely delineated term that might ensure a certain amount of communication; but it would differ from true wisdom, the living symbol of peoples' wisdom traditions. These traditions do not refer to a term fixed in content but to an integrated experience which people have named. Perhaps this process could compare to a lover's naming the beloved. It is possible that the word "wisdom" is already so worn out that it no longer conveys this love experience to us. One might substitute the word "beauty" for the word "wisdom," for example. When arriving at a certain level of experience and language, one starts inventing—without wanting to play God—a certain *coincidentia oppositorum,* an interplay of opposites, a convergence of all senses. One discovers that there cannot be justice without love, beauty without justice, wisdom without beauty; without prudence everything vanishes. Therefore, wisdom is a living symbol here, backed by a certain consensus among traditions; but it cannot be reduced to a mere concept.

Wisdom is not insensitive; therefore, it is not always victorious. Wisdom encompasses mercy—buddhists would call it *karunā,* empathy, as in "sharing one's destiny." Wisdom is not blind to the person's well-being. At the same time, wisdom cannot be reduced to the negative, painful sides of reality. It cannot be overcome by the debris and suffering of this world.

At times, one encounters people—not only in Asia or Africa but also here—who have integrated misfortune or suffering into their lives with an incredible, sovereign serenity; they have dealt with suffering and have settled with it in such a way that they have gained, in spite of this negative side of life, a fountain of joy, depth, peace, and empathy. It is wisdom that enables us not to despair of suffering and to bear the negative aspects of human existence and the injustices of our society, everything that should make us really revolt. Wisdom enables us not to give up good faith, hope, and even joy. When retracting to mere terminology, one opposite excludes the other. When having to endure suffering, I cannot feel joy. Yet there is a mystical coexistence of these opposites in our lives that cannot be explained rationally, in spite of all the dark sides of life, of the environment, of one's personal history. We all carry the responsibility for everything that ever occurred in the universe. Having transcended one's personal individualism just a little, one can cope with the suffering and pain of this world. This overcoming of suffering is part of wisdom.

In this chapter, I mentioned alchemy, a transformation, a metamorphosis, which will take place in us when we welcome reality with open arms just because it has *arrived*. This welcome constitutes neither a naïve optimism nor a desperate pessimism; it is neither a senselessly screaming protest nor a fatalistic surrender. The kind of being I mean is an activity; but this activity is free and we participate in its freedom. True wisdom is the source of this activity, of this metamorphosis. Under its influence I am well aware that my action will always be one-sided. When finally taking a certain direction, I know well enough what I truly should do. But if another person takes a different direction, I will welcome it, because only with such polarities does life stay lively.

Is the church a dwelling place for wisdom?[36]
That depends on us!

II. *Quaternitas Perfecta:*
The Fourfold Nature of Man

This is its magnificence, and even greater is Man:
One fourth of it constitutes all living things, three fourths of it
constitute the eternal things of heaven. Purusha-sūkta.
Rig Veda X, 90, 3

In this chapter we will observe more closely what the human dwelling place of wisdom looks like. It requires that we meditate on our true self. We are not talking here about a certain picture of Man, as generated by the various human cultures of the world in both theory and practice in their respectively distinct ways. We are talking here about something that *preceded* these developments and interpretations and therefore finds expression in most peoples through their particular traditions.

In order to describe this original insight, we cannot limit ourselves to a single tradition's language and thought. This would mean equating the world of this one tradition with the universe at large, thereby making its view of Man a blueprint for all others. Yet at the same time we must avoid an artificial dilution of the various traditions that attempts, for unity's sake, to impose a common denominator. Such a dilution would have to omit all the elements of each tradition that could not be made to agree with the others, so that in the end only common platitudes devoid of life would be left. A third difficulty is that many people today are no longer familiar with the tradition of their ancestors. Modern life itself has already caused a certain dilution of the past, perhaps not in its most profound archetypes but certainly in the kind of superficial existence most people live today. This is the case not only in the West, for example, in the christian countries, but also in similar fashion in Africa, India, Japan, and in most other parts of the world and in their religions. To be sure, there are groups everywhere wanting to counter the impending secularism and syncretism by means of a revival and a stabilization of their own respective traditions. But this dilution has already taken place, and an artificial fundamentalism can only be a body brace, not the spine of a living body, regardless of whether one calls it humanity, "Body of Christ," "*dharmakāya,*" or something else.

How can we create a language that is not exclusive but still concrete, that is simple to understand but still thorough? It would have to respect the various traditions as such and also avoid stumbling over the obstacles we have mentioned. If there is such a language, it must be found in the basic human condition as we see it in a large part of humanity: What characterizes us? What makes us human? These are the most general but at the same time the most concrete questions we should discuss and ponder here.

I have dealt with this subject from the viewpoints of traditional anthropologies, thereby developing the concept of a *quaternitas perfecta,* a fourfold image of the human being.[1]

I may recall here the famous verse 25 of *The Golden Verses of Pythagoras:*

> I swear it by the One who in our hearts engraved
> The sacred Tetrad, symbol immense and pure,
> Source of Nature and model of the Gods. *

This sacred quaternary was well known to the christian scholastics who approved of it; see for instance Hugh of St. Victor in his *Didascalicon,* I, 11. **

As a matter of fact this symbol of the quaternitas may be found in various western, eastern, and southern traditions. Each of these traditions uses a set of symbols and terms: for example, in greek antiquity the words *sôma, psychê, polis, aiôn;* in India the words *jīva, aham, ātman,* and *brahman;* and in many archaic traditions (of which we are also reminded by western esoterics) the words *earth, water, fire,* and *air.* With the help of these symbols, we will speak of four centers, thereby placing basic human traits in their midst. We will assign to each of these centers certain symbols. For each I have

---

*The translation is from Nayán Louise Redfield, who rendered into english *The Golden Verses of Pythagoras,* explained and translated into french by Fabre d'Olivet, London (Putnam's Sons) 2nd. ed. 1925.

**Didascalicon de studio legendi,* PL 176, 739 ff. There is a critical edition by Ch. H. Buttimer, Washington 1939.

chosen an element in nature, a word from greek and indic anthropologies, a human possibility, a philosophical phenomenon, a state of human activity, and an anthropological area. The symbols proper to each center are not simply interchangeable; *sôma* is not *jīva,* and *aiôn* is not *brahman.* The *quaternitas* as a whole constitutes a *homeomorphic* structure, a unified system that has in each of the examined traditions its respective function and meaning. (This structure will be depicted in the chart at the end of the chapter.)

We are primarily concerned with the basic dignity of Man, because the person is a microcosm, a representation of the whole, a spark of the never-ceasing fire. This cross-cultural image of Man could enable us to overcome the split of reality that so painfully tortures and threatens modernity. This image could transform the various dualities (*dvandva*)—resulting from a destructive break between Man and the Earth, the subject and the object, understanding and love, arts and sciences, masculine and feminine—into creative polarities. This would be true also for the final break of reality, the one between Man and God, time and eternity, or creator and creation. The *quaternitas perfecta* gives us a chance to discover an adequate human spirituality; it is the basis for a new spiritual attitude of the person to self, to the other, to the environment, and also to the all-embracing reality called God in many traditions.

What should we do? How should we act? How should we apply ourselves and behave? Not just since Kant, but also since the beginnings of philosophical meditation, certain ethical questions have emerged in both western and eastern traditions. Humanity is seeking a solution to these questions when giving different, but ultimately homeomorphic answers. Yet even more basic are the questions: Why should I *have to*? Why should I ask for an *ought*? Why should I ask myself at all what to do? A danger lies hidden here. Life is filled with dangers, and we have to face up to them, not circumvent them or avoid them. The danger here is called quietism, fatalism, regress into irrational behavior. We must not forget than in human life both nature and culture are intimately related. Not only nature is involved in Man; the human being also has a cultural makeup. One must emphasize that. But at the same time one should not lose joy and spontaneity when trying to overcome danger. To begin with we should try to embrace the whole as the whole; or, to say it differently, we should try to experience the nakedness of life. We must discover the center, which so often has been covered up by all kinds of activities.

One could try to overcome the question of why we should be concerned with the *ought* by taking a third step: Why should I do something? Why should I have to? Why should I even have to ask this second why?—One could go on like this forever. When innocence has been lost at one point, when the why has popped up, further questions cannot be repressed. Yet ultimately such questions lead nowhere.

If we want to solve a problem, we must face the problem and stop going in the opposite direction. There is a human attitude for that, which I call the new (not the second) innocence. It *believes* that it has touched on a basic ground so that any further questions become unnecessary. With our anthropological *quaternitas* I hope to have touched on this ground in our time so that we can stand on it firmly. In other words, what I am trying to present is a certain synthesis, a distillation, an essence contained in a variety of human traditions.

The *quaternitas,* the fourfoldness, represents this wholeness of which we have already spoken under different names and aspects. First we will concentrate on one center of this fourfoldness and then on the other centers. The reason for this *concentration,* this focusing in, is to bring together under the one aspect all given facts, the entire manifoldness of the world, and to retrace these conditions each time to one center without any forms of reductionism. This process will take place for each of the four centers, so that we experience them all in a *concentric* fashion. Thus, a human life would be able to overcome the ruptures, the schizophrenia, the tensions, and the painful torments by which it so often is marked. Wise is the one who, in a concentric way, experiences and lives out these four centers. The circles around each of the centers are not identical since body is not soul and soul not all of reality. But both body and soul are concentric, so that the center of the world goes right through the middle of my soul as well as my body.

Speaking without any introductory explanations about such fundamental, difficult questions may not be appropriate; perhaps I have been influenced by the western need for acceleration. But if anything is worth doing, it may be worth doing in an imperfect manner too. Thus I dare to take on the *quaternitas perfecta* since it is something that affects us all as both human beings and creatures and since it is an essential ingredient of reality.

There are some difficulties here: first, the difficulties of my own language; second, the particular difficulties of today's languages in trying, especially here, to express the relevant conditions and experiences; third, the difficulty of language at large. Furthermore, I cannot do justice to this integrated anthropology, since not all symbols are thoroughly discussed. Our intent is to point distinctly to the seat of wisdom, where, according to christian tradition, Mary is seated (*sedes sapientiae*). This seat is a symbol of the unmarred basic human nature, and we do not want to leave Mary there all by herself. Mary's calling is the destiny of Man in general. Otherwise, there would not have been a revolution among the angels in heaven. But Man, who has a seat there too, is supposed to be fully human, *Adam, purusha.* It is this kind of full humanness we want to discuss—and, for the moment, not its particulars.

First Center: Earth and Body

What is the first dimension? It is represented by such symbols as Earth, *sôma* or *jīva* (body, individuality), *karman* (doing), *bonum* (the good), being awake, and includes the area of morality.

Sôma and Jīva: We are body; we do not simply have a body. We are individuals; we do not only have individuality. We are active individuals; we not only exercise certain activities. We are earth; we not only are gravitating on a planet, not only are living in a country, not only are standing on this earth as if it were just a platform. As long as we do not overcome our separateness from matter and are not healing this break, as long as we regard bodily activity or *yoga* simply as a technical exercise and the body in one extreme as an enemy and in the other as a ruler, we will not have lived to the fullest potential as human beings. We will remain torn. Eventually it all will take vengeance, not only in terms of health or activity but also in terms of inner dissatisfaction and restlessness.

Our meditation could also be called *practical introduction to spiri-*

tuality. The word spirituality has both good and bad connotations. It circumvents aspects of doctrine usually connected with the word religion. Spirituality is not yet too much marred by dogmatic differentiations and intellectual subtleties. Furthermore, the word has the advantage that it ignores the view that the various religions are self-enclosed, as if separated by fixed, old boundaries. There is, for example, a spirituality of love or of political involvement that pours through all the various religions. At the same time, however, the word "spirituality" has a negative connotation, since it seems to deal with the "spirit," the mind, and perhaps to neglect everything else. But this would be the wrong kind of spirituality; it would have lost its relatedness to matter, to the earth.

We are primarily body, individual, Earth. Connected with this relatedness to body and earth are activity, action, and *karman*. We *are* these individuals, these bodily beings, these active subjects; the state of being awake is essentially part of what we are. Only because of that are we able to feel, to sense, and to experience.

Earth: "Earth" means matter; it could be a stone, a tree, a mountain, a house, my finger—going further, perhaps also a machine, a car, an airplane. We must not draw back from Earth. One might refer in a probably poor exegetical exercise to the Bible, for example, Genesis I:28, "making the Earth subject to us." But if we do so in a sovereign, elitist way (thus, making ourselves the generous kings), presuming to dominate the Earth intellectually and believing that we understand it better, our human vanity may be satisfied for a time. Ultimately, however, this is not enough—for our human need for wholeness, for collaborating in the fulfillment of the Earth's destiny and participating in the destiny of the universe remains unfulfilled. As urgent and as necessary as short-term solutions may be, the basic problems require a much more in-depth treatment. We must start with the realization that the break between the "it" and the "we" has to be mended; we, too, are Earth.

As long as I do not regard every piece of mere Earth as my own body, I not only disregard the Earth but also misunderstand my body. Understanding begins at this point! All scientific and anthropological inventions (and imaginations) about the human being have arrived only later—proteins, chromosomes, alpha waves, and so on.

For thousands of years, people have not been schizophrenic, have had full awareness of their personalities without fathoming any of our physiology, biology, and chemistry. All of these may be necessary, nice, and useful today, but, anthropologically speaking, these findings are simply accidental paraphernalia, something dispensable for reaching the fullness of human existence. Modern sciences might even become hindrances after a certain time; certainly they are unnecessary for enjoying and attaining the fullness of human nature. Concerning humanness, we moderns are in no way exceptional just by being westerners, first-class passengers on this planet.

Earth, body, *yoga,* waking; having a normal state of consciousness, an awareness of our individuality—all these are essentially human and real. We are real only when we *are* all the above. If I have to take a dance class to learn the turning of my body or the art of motion, then something of my humanness is missing. If I have to consult a book to tell me that the trees are pretty and only then look out the window to confirm that, then I am not yet fully human. (This is not to criticize books or dance classes; what matters is the way we use them and our body.) We must return and develop an attitude where true human (not just animal-like) spontaneity becomes possible, where we can again learn, talk, see, enjoy from within.

One can hardly assume that flowers think of, reflect on, and imagine how beautiful they are. And we are more than flowers, as the Gospel states (Matt. VI:30). If we want human beauty to become a reality to us, we have to learn from the bud's bringing forth the flower—without strain or force, in the proper rhythm, and in its own time. The Gospel says that we should *look at* the lilies of the field and at the birds in the sky and not ponder over them or take them home to see them better. Our culture should be at least as natural as the nature of a flower. Violence sets in only when our cultures are unnatural. Struggle is a natural state, but not war. Hunting may belong to human nature, but not what modern societies are doing. They are artificially accumulating food and turning it into a weapon. In fact, we should not need laws to tell us that the production of arms is against human rights. But our idea of the human being and our ethical thinking concerning arms have not gone as far as they have concerning cannibalism, which our sensitivity perceives as a transgression against humanness.

Karman, Bonum, and Morality: Individual action and external activity—we are that too, though not exclusively. A western master—someone from the Rhineland, Meister Eckhart—speaks of three veils that are hiding reality from us as the coat hides the body. He mentions these veils in an exposition of Romans VIII:18 (LW IV, 11, 2).[2] The biblical passage speaks of *revelatio,* revelation (which really means an "unveiling") of glory, of splendor, of *"gloria."* We shall mention here the first veil. Eckhart calls it *"velamen boni,"* the veil of the good, the moral. It is a thick veil: everything on Earth is protected by the veil of the good and threatened by evil. Everything is evaluated under the categories of good and evil. Whatever it is we want to accomplish, we want it *sub specie boni,* under the aspect of good. I do something *because* it is good! I want it *because* its purpose is good—whatever its good may be. We become active because we envision a good goal. *"Voluntas videtur quasi mercennaria,"* Eckhart says, "the will appears as a hired servant."

The good not only moves human existence; it also leads all levels of existence. We may be a little more perfect than an animal offered a piece of food. We may be more attracted by splendor, a piece of truth, a revelation of beauty, something we envision, something we have to, or want to, accomplish. The good is very powerful, but ultimately it is only a cover.

The veil of the good has to do with the will. Only under this veil's protection, so says Eckhart, is the will able to "comprehend" (God). Revelation is the unveiling of this splendor; it is the removing of the veil that covers everything governed by good (and evil, as its counterpart) and, therefore, belongs to the kingdom of the will. Schelling has said: "The will is the primordial being."[3] Here we find the opposite: the will is only an appearance of being. Humanity, having believed in this will to power and the power of the will, has accomplished great things through this belief. The will is the engine, the power that moves us. Modern pedagogy tells us that we have to have a goal and a strong will, and that we have to use the will for reaching the goal. Yet we have produced a worship of the will as a result. The will has become our biggest commodity; we are no longer able to imagine life without goal, purpose, and will. Often we even reach these goals and meet our plans. All great empires of history and all great human accomplishments are wonderful testimonies to the fruit of the will of a person or a people. Surveying thousands of years of human experience, however, we see that such glamour also has its dark side, that the price to be paid for such testimonies of our culture is the exploitation and subjection of other peoples and even of other parts of our own personality.

The will is usually directed toward action, the *karman,* activity. The will's field is morality, the moral life. The will "wills" to dominate human reality. It reigns in the areas of the individual, the bodily, and the earthly; among the four seasons, it corresponds to summer. All these areas are governed by the will. But if we want to overcome one-sidedness, we must learn *concentration,* by which we shall reach a center in this incredibly complicated territory of the will. Our journey there cannot be through twisting the truth, resentment, repression, or developing an even stricter will or an even stronger unwillingness. The journey consists in *being concentrated.* One cannot go against the will without being taken again by the power of the will. Wisdom cannot be a fruit of the will, as we have already seen. Only by being centered is the will placed where it belongs.

Harmony of Action: There is one criterion for this center (I could mention many witnesses from the most varied religious traditions to make my case). According to St. Ignatius of Loyola, this criterion is the *indifferentia sancta,* the "blessed indifference," a certain calmness, a sovereign composure toward things.[4] Expressing it in our words, the characteristic of the center, of the central point, is its equidistance from all points on the circumference. This is the kind of indifference we are concerned with; it was called "equanimity" by the ancients, but not indifference. The buddhist tradition calls it *upekshā (upekkhā).*

It would be the wrong kind of indifference—though one that is found quite frequently—if it did not allow me to become enthusiastic, excited, if it did not permit me to get involved in something my heart aspires toward and to take steps against something I consider bad or inhumane. But it means, on the other hand, a loss of the middle, an absolutizing that slips into fanaticism when I worship this emotion, this movement of the mind and self, to the point that everything depends only on winning the battle. When I am "centered," I do not lose the center—which cannot be lost anyway. It is then that I attain equanimity, a balance and an inner strength that permit me to risk my life without making everything dependent on the victory of my efforts: There is much more in human life than victories!

But here too lurks a vice into which equanimity can slip. This vice is sluggishness, the lack of enthusiasm, of interest, of engagement, and of vitality. As always, true wisdom consists of the proper balance; one can reach this balance by means of contemplation. Of course, it takes a certain adroitness, and at this point I introduce the word "harmony." The search for the center is not a crusade. Harmony can develop only when emerging by itself. One cannot force its evolution. Nowhere should a sign of violence be present, especially not inner violence. The confucian tradition teaches that when a gong is well forged, you can hit it as much as you want to, with whatever you want to, on the side or in the middle, in a good or in a bad mood—the sound issuing from it will always remain pure and harmonic. It is the kind of harmony that does not depend on externals but simply is; it has no need of propaganda.

The reality of nature, and especially of human nature, is like a net, a great wealth of distinct influences that in the end come together in one whole—we are *jīva,* individual creatures. Therefore, we need to identify ourselves with our bodies, with our "Earth." Alchemy and the traditional teachings of the elements had their source in such a form of identification, not in a physical curiosity about how the Earth rotated, about how heavy or dense something was, or things like that. Even without Newton's law of gravity, it is possible to discover that one's body and a stone are related to weight and are similar in this respect.

The Veil of the Good: How can I make this veil of the good transparent in such a delicate way as not to tear it, as not to forget both good and evil? How can I recognize it as a veil, leaving it the way it is, discovering it eventually as being a tool of revelation, of an "unveiling"? Meister Eckhart writes: "Not by adding, but by subtracting, God is found in the soul . . . because God is innermost in the soul, and the creature can only contribute by means of one's own cleansing and preparing" (LW IV, II,2). The answer lies not in denying good and evil but in overcoming the two. Yet we have to realize that both good and evil are only external veils that do not touch the naked creature or pure reality. In the indic tradition, the lotus is the symbol of this untouched state of cleanness.

Indra is a Vedic God who—as a scandal to some indologists—stands beyond good and evil, not because he commits moral crimes (then he would not be beyond evil) but because he has torn the veil. Certainly, this is highly dangerous and discomfiting! But when actions are simply patterned after a certain model, they cannot be free. Perhaps only a God can afford to do without the model—or a new human innocence can. Perhaps this is what christians call *theôsis*.

In this center are united *equidistance* and simultaneous participation in all things. The question is how to allow my identity to grow to the point where I can identify with both my body and the entire Earth; at the same time I will remain distant from everything and will not absolutize it. In order to do this I need experience, which I gather with my own body. Even headaches and stomach problems are part of experience, and they should not lead me to despair. On the contrary, I discover that, though I *am* what I experience, I am not *solely* that. After all, what I am is *my* own being, and this being is what constitutes my identity. Being is a verb and cannot be turned into a subject, let alone into an object. When we allow "our" being to penetrate our body and the "earth," we can then enjoy its freedom in us, which would mean that we have overcome the "ought."

I began this chapter with the questions, What should I do? What should I think? This overcoming of the ought cannot be sincere when we simultaneously neglect the other little word of this classic formulation: What should *I* do and think? It leads us to the second center of our *quaternitas*. The overcoming of the I—which means, paradoxically, the overcoming of any identification of the I. This can happen only when complexity is not repressed but is assimilated and embodied in such a way as to leave room for further assimilation and embodiment. "The sage acts without making decisions," Chuang-tzu says (II,9).[5]

Second Center: Water and Self

The second dimension in which we exist, which allows us to exist, without which our life would fade away, has once again various symbols, described differently in the various traditions. Each of these symbols focuses on one of this dimensions's aspects: water, *psychê* (soul), *aham* (I), *jñāna* (knowledge, understanding, reason), *verum* (truth), dreaming, the psychological aspect in the deepest sense of the word. Just as we are *jīva, sôma,* Earth, so we are all the above.

We will examine now four of these symbols. We may suspect the importance of *water* comes from the fact that our bodies consist of more than 70 percent water. But we are "water" also in another sense. In the same way, we not only have but also are *knowledge, understanding, reason.* This is not meant in an abstract sense. After all, we are *aham,* "I." And we are *truth* inasmuch as we are looking for it. All these symbols are pointing directly to *the other,* to this otherness (of ourselves), to the *alius* and not only to the *aliud,* to the strange, to the Non-I. There is no I without a Thou; there is no isolated and individually existing soul in the least respect, no individual life. Water and understanding are symbols of relationship. We exist and live in a web of relationships. We become aware of ourselves when becoming aware of others.

This second dimension of the *quaternitas* has something to do with patience. As the Gospel of Luke says: We will only live and gain our lives in patience (Luke XXI:19). Patience is synonymous with tolerance—at least, this is the case with the greek word *hypomonê* in this Gospel (Luke VIII:15). We can recognize this also in the symbol of water: water is tolerance; any sort of container is sufficient, big or small, it does not matter. Water nestles against anything; it adjusts, endures everything, has no special preference, is not edgy, not solid; it always gives in. One can—if one does it right—jump into water from a height of many feet; water still adapts.

Water: The symbolic power of water lies, first of all, in the fact that it flows, that it refreshes, that it makes life possible, and that it can trickle away. But something else exists, in addition, of which we have lost sight (here various wisdom traditions of Africa become important). Water is not only the source of life but is life itself. Water *is* life. Therefore, such phrases as "the water of life" or "the water of eternal life" (see John IV:14) should not be understood in a figurative sense only. The fact that we cannot exist without water is more than a mere game of ideas. Even the polarity between the water's dynamics and flowing, on the one hand, and its stillness, on the other, does not yet exhaust the symbol. (In some traditions water symbolizes the spiritual pilgrimage: flowing, bubbling water means *life,* while water quiet as a mirror becomes a symbol of self-discovery.) Water is life; thus its characteristics are those of life itself.

On the Tuesday after Easter, people sang in the latin liturgy: "The water of wisdom he gave them," in reference to Sirach XV:3. The *Atharva Veda* sings, "Why do the waters, flowing toward truth, never stop flowing?" (X,7,37). According to many traditions, including the jewish, the waters were not created (Gen. I:2). Water is "the medicinal drink for immortality" (SB IV,4,3,15) and the lap of God (SB VI,8,2,4). Water is the source of man. The chinese word (*ch'üan* consists of the signs "pure" and "water"; similarly, the latin word *fons* (spring) means origin.

Jñāna: Understanding means intellectual understanding of what is given, of what is present. "All that is understood, is understood by something already present." With this sentence Bonaventure sums up in his own occidental language what many traditions hold.[6] Be it in the *parousia* of the greek, the *pramāna* of indic philosophy, or the distinctions of the present (whether *prae-sensu, praes-ens, prae-essentia . . .*) and present reality, *présence* and *trace,* all of them point out the *in-between.* Christ is supposed to have said: "The kingdom of God is *between* you" ("in the midst of," *entos,* Luke XVII:21); or, as the Gospel of Thomas says: "The kingdom is inside of you and outside of you" (logion 3). As it may be, the human being is a creature for whom reality as a whole is present. Therefore, Man is also knowledge and understanding.

Knowledge is not only knowledge *about* something; understanding does not simply mean to be familiar with something (or being able to do something, being in command of something or having power over it). When viewing knowledge solely as a refined hunt for information, for laws, for some sort of objects, we are, in reality, still thinking in a very unrefined manner. Not only do women not want to be objects for men—and vice versa; things in general have begun protesting against being treated as mere "sex objects," that is, objects of understanding. We are slowly learning to regard animals seriously as sensing creatures. Thus, the protest arises against cold-blooded experimenting on animals in research laboratories. But the point goes further: As brutal as animal testing is, even things are crying out: Stop treating us as mere objects (of exploitation; or, resources). Respect for life entails respect for *all* beings.

The need for manipulative experiments for the sake of gaining insight and under the pretense of utility is, culturally speaking, a pathological need. Certainly one can extricate many insights from nature that way, just as one can squeeze out confessions by torturing someone; it is always useful—for the dominating party, "the powers that be." But one should not seek comfort in the thought that frogs or amoebas are suffering less because of a little anesthesia. Theoretical puritanism is not the point here; the basic attitude underlying it is. Native Americans used to ask trees for forgiveness before cutting them down. Alchemists used to trace the deeper relationships of various elements with each other and the dynamics of God's creation. Astrology used to investigate—in spite of many aberrations— the interrelatedness of all occurrences in the cosmos. In their actions, all these groups preserved their respect for creation. Today it is different. Yet we cannot simply revert to these traditions of human history. Rather, we are dealing here with a "return," which—as almost all traditions suggest—begins with a turning inward.

Here it is especially important to critique the most relevant method of today's sciences, the experiment. The experiment is not a path to wisdom; it presupposes a distorted image of Man. We do not want to discuss here the so-called problem of knowing in western philosophy (or what indic philosophy calls *pramāna*)—the means, that is, of true knowing, such as conclusion, attestation, cognition, and the like. Nor are we criticizing each human intervention (which actually means "mediation") in nature. Instead we are discussing the term understanding as denoting an intervention in the enclosure of being. In order to do so, we have to distinguish the experiment from experience and observation.

Understanding Through Experience, Observation, and Experiment: Experience means allowing something to directly affect and penetrate me. It means absorbing it so I can identify with what I have come to understand. The person's ability of understanding is nothing but the ability of identification—the fact that we can become *everything*. In the western tradition, Aristotle has said: "The soul *is* everything, so to speak" (*De anima* III,8; 431b,21), primarily because the soul is able to know everything. This sentence was also one of the pillars of medieval ontology until epistemology became severed from the former. Similarly, the *upanishads* say: "One becomes what one understands"; "whoever understands *brahman*, becomes *brahman*" (MundU III,2,9,3B). This is not a *circulus vitiosus* but a *circulus vitalis*, a circle of life.

Experience is full of risk. Only what has been experienced can be interpreted; only then can one understand it. Only what has penetrated me and then springs out of me in a spontaneous fashion, has life, power, and authority. One might explain this more precisely in philosophical language. Buddhist logic even says that the principle of identity is not poignant enough for upholding true understanding, because the identity between the one who understands and what has been understood is greater than the identity of the logical principle of identity. Thomas Aquinas would agree.

But one could also explain it differently: During the 1920s or early 1930s a simple woman came to see Mahātmā Gandhi in his ashram in Ahmadabad, asking him: "Bapujī, would you, please, tell my child not to eat so many sweets! I've told her so many times it is bad for the teeth!" Gandhi remained silent and did not say a word. The mother looked down. She thought she had said something inappropriate and retreated in embarrassment. A few months later, she came back to the ashram, and there was the opportunity for a follow-up—it was now more out of curiosity than motherly love. She asked why Gandhi had not answered her before. "You know, my daughter," said Gandhi, "at that time I liked eating sweets myself too much. My words would not have had any impact!"

Sermons not lived out and loved and completely internalized and words not stemming from one's personal life cannot be powerful. How can I tell the little girl "Don't eat sweets!" if I eat sweets myself? How can I dare say a word, if I have not created, lived, endured, discovered it earlier myself? Every person understands this logic. Experience as a path to understanding, as an identification with what has been understood, is a sacramental intertwining of the person with the things one understands. This way we grow, mature, live.

In the case of experience, identity is complete: I am what I understand. But we do not understand *everything* in life by means of experience. For example, a smoker does not understand the harmfulness of smoking by experience. One can get information from others, know of statistics on lung cancer, and so forth. But as soon as I experience that smoking is not beneficial to my body, I quit—unless I want to harm my body intentionally. If I continue in spite of it, that means I do not really understand that smoking is ultimately harmful to me in this experiential way. Instead it is pseudo-knowledge, knowledge by hear-say.

But there is a second way of understanding, which differs from experience and presupposes a certain distinction between the one who understands and what has been understood. It is called *observation*. In the case of experience, everything penetrates me; perhaps I cannot stand that and would collapse under the force, the intensity, the power of experience. Observation is different; it is a paradoxical thing. For one it can be described as a "passive activity," requiring attention and consideration; for another it can be described as a consent to be influenced, to be reached by the outside, even to be attacked at times. Understanding in the form of observation is not yet identical with what is, in a stricter sense, meant by understanding in most western languages: recognizing, realizing, comprehending. There is a possible wordplay in english: to understand means to "stand under." One does not stand above, as we commonly might see it; instead one is subdued by the matter one understands. That is observation.

In order to be able to observe, one does not need to identity with the matter or the thing observed. One need not become a fish, a titmouse. One simply has to be present and wait until the (un)expected appears. But one must not expect too intensely, or else one becomes nervous and disturbs the observation. One need only wait. When the animal comes, the revelation arrives, the thing begins to move, then one must not become violent; one waits, anticipates, observes, remains passive, leaves initiative up to the other, the thing (not the *objectum* one can "thrust forward"). It is then that one learns and understands. It takes time, and one is subject to a thing's moods; one is dependent on the freedom of reality on whose rhythms one must not impinge. Actually, observation (*observatio*) means preserving (*servare*) a situation the way it is. A more philosophical name for this conscious acceptance of a present situation would be perception: we perceive what is facing us.

In this way, by means of experience and observation, each person gains understanding. Children have experiences the moment they are born. As we grow, our ability to observe increases continually. Experience can become dangerous, observation disappointing; experience requires an open mind, observation patience.

Modern science prefers a third method of understanding. It is the *experiment.* It consists in altering, in a more or less artificial way, at least one variable in an observable system and then assessing the alteration of the system at large. The experiment makes possible the calculation of variation and variables and is at the same time built on this calculation. One can list the various steps of this calculation; one can plan ahead. Experience requires long preparation, observation an empathic adaptation to the rhythms of nature. But the experiment is supposedly more practical and gains quicker results than the other two. Experience penetrates me; in observation I have to participate—but the experiment runs "on the side"; I just have to check once in a while what has happened.

Francis Bacon, who in this modern sense is called the father of the experiment, speaks explicitly of the aim of controlling nature (*Novum Organum* I,70ff.). Before his time, the word experiment had almost the same meaning as *experientia,* experience. Strictly speaking, one would have to distinguish between experiments and measurements, but both are closely related.

I suggest that this third kind of understanding is an abnormal kind—in what true understanding is concerned with. One does not really come to understand the thing itself. One simply gets to know a certain reaction of a certain matter within determined parameters. The experiment is primarily an opportunity for controlling, for calculating, perhaps for previewing and influencing. It only offers information concerning a certain course of events, but it does not say much about the nature of things, about reality, about our own nature. Even a child explores this method of understanding when experimenting with toys—but after that, one cannot play with these toys again in the same way because the experiment has turned the toy into pieces; it has altered the nature of things. By this kind of method, one might gain power, prestige, money, and much else, perhaps even contentedness—fascinating things, without doubt. But understanding in its true sense cannot be gained this way. One fits reality into a system of thought, not the other way around.

The distinctions between experience, observation, and experiment should not be understood as separations. All three methods of understanding are often intertwined and even show some hierarchical structure. Ultimately, the experiment needs observation, which has to turn into a certain experience so we can gain understanding. There is no pure experiment but also no pure experience.

Aham: An intimate relationship exists between the I and the Thou. German idealism could turn itself inside out, if it were to introduce a dialogue between the I and the Thou, rather than maintaining its dialectic between the I and the Non-I. But idealism is certainly correct in saying that the Non-I is not the I, but rather its opposite. Based on that, one can logically divide reality into the spheres of the I and the Non-I, a split that consequently leads to absolute idealism. But the Thou is neither I nor Non-I. The relationship between the Thou and the I is neither the dialectic relationship between the Non-I and the I nor a relationship between the I and itself. This is nothing culturally specific, but a common human experience that each child has. Unfortunately, modern languages have completely lost the dual (as opposed to the plural), which exemplifies this twofoldness in terms of grammar. In sanskrit, arabic, and greek, on the other hand, it is preserved.

In this context, I dare make a more general comment: I am under the impression that we are practicing language genocide. Not only do we kill trees but also human languages. In this century alone, over one thousand languages have disappeared. If that continues, it will take less than one century for the majority of today's five thousand languages to become extinct. Languages are not only tools, but each language constitutes a world—not only a worldview. Each language is a wealth of human life. Not only animal species are rendered extinct; hundreds of human heroic characters and myths are also disappearing or are close to extinction. The reason for their waning is that we have assaulted the languages as if they were simply means of information, like satellites or radios.

We come back now to the singular, dual, and plural. In our language, there is no grammatical form expressing the I-and-Thou. That would be the dual. The dual has great power; it is not the plural but presupposes a Thou, thus forming a "higher" entity. This fact has been quite impressively described by Ferdinand Ebner, Martin Buber, and others.[7] The Thou constitutes the addressability of the person, Ebner says. The "in-between"–person (*Zwischen mensch*) is the true person, Buber says. "If there is no [any] other person (or thing), there is no I," one can hear already Chuang-tzu say (II,2).[8] The in-between is the dual, that which overcomes the "Thou-lessness" (Ebner) of the I.

The dual reflects the discovery that the I needs a Thou, which is different in nature from a third, the It, and from all others. The dual is an experience, and its disappearance is a revealing example of the change of human behavior. Whether or not we call each other by first names (because we have become a little familiar) has very little to do with it. It has to do with something else, namely, with the experience of the I, impossible without the experience of the Thou. And this Thou need not be only the "beloved Thou of my heart"; it can also be something threatening. But it is a part of me without which I am unable to live. It is something that can challenge, endanger, love, somehow change me, and which rescues me from my proud loneliness. Many a person's rescue may be found in owning a cat or a dog. It is better than nothing but certainly cannot be a model for this I-Thou relationship. For one's reflecting on self, for being oneself, *aham,* the Thou without which there is no I, is needed.

The Thou is not something I choose. Indian sociologists are very proud of the fact that the indian custom of arranged marriages is, despite its "primitivity," proving apparently more successful than the western range of marriage options and choices. In India, the discovery of the Thou is not a question of individual choice and decision. "I marry the woman I love"—"I love the woman I marry": this is the usual formula for differentiating. Certainly, it also depends on one's faith or superstition, one's tradition or routine. Here in the west, it would be objectionable if we wanted to introduce such a (at least nowadays) foreign system. This is not my intention. I am only attempting to understand the differences. Because ultimately, we are talking about the bare experience of life—an experience, standing apart from such cultural or historical differences, but still not separated from them.

Psychê, Dreaming, and Verum: Speaking of *psychē,* I could mention zen meditation, which attempts to help us lead our *psychē* to quietude. Mentioning zen might be enough at this point. Concerning the symbol of dreaming (in the truest sense of the word), one would have to discuss depth psychology, but also the *Māndūkya Upanishad.* If the danger in the first dimension is sluggishness, here it is intellectualism, the urge to examine things by means of experiments and not to understand them by observation and experience.

If, according to Meister Eckhart, the temptation and, simultaneously, the task of the first dimension is to overcome the *velamen boni,* the "veil of the good," the temptation of the second is the *velamen veri,* the "veil of the true." Just as the will can only function under the veil of the good, the intellect can only function under the veil of the true. If the first dimension carries with it the danger of placing everything under the will, the second holds the danger of using the intellect solely. One should insert an observation here parallel to our remarks concerning the first center: one must not neglect reason; one must not forget truth—but reality cannot be reduced to intelligibility, to "thinkability." Reality is not *only* truth. In reference to Dionysius, Bonaventure says: "The highest form of reality is called darkness because the intellect does not comprehend it."[9]

History seems to show that people committed the most horrid acts in the name of truth. One could argue on phenomenological grounds that truth is always what one is *looking for.* But one cannot argue that what one *finds* is always truth. What one is looking for may very well be truth, but what one finds may *not* be truth. When insisting on knowing the truth, one has already destroyed truth in one's soul, since wisdom no longer resides in it. As Thomas Aquinas teaches, it is a paradox to insist on holding the truth; it can, at the most, hold us. Truth is always only a cover, and that means ultimately that we cannot identify truth with reality at large. As soon as we touch truth, it becomes infected by all our shortcomings; thereby the truth that is supposed to set us free becomes our captive. How could it set us free then?

This does not mean that we cannot rely on truth. It only means that truth itself is merely a cover for reality, and needed cover so that being can become visible to us. Truth is the visibility of being, as far as being is intelligible. But the person must meet this revelation, this unveiling, halfway and, after meeting it, must be prepared to live on in this bottomless abyss of mystery. *Ungrund,* says Meister Eckhart (DW III,36; etc.).

Third Center: Fire and Being

For the first dimension of the *quaternitas* I have chosen the name "waking"; for the second "dreaming" (here lies a deep irony in the nature of being, on which I cannot elaborate further: dreaming corresponds to thinking and reasoning). The third dimension is connected with "sleeping" in the classical sense of indic philosophy (*sushupti*). If the first dimension is called *jîva* and the second *aham,* then the third is called *ātman.* If in the first we are speaking of *sôma* and in the second of *psychê,* then we are speaking here in the third of *polis.* If the symbol of the first is the Earth and of the second the Water, then in the third it is Fire. And if the first level is *karman* and the second is *jñāna,* then the third is *bhakti.* If the center of the first dimension is the moral and of the second the psychological, then the center of the third is the ontic. We are fire, *polis* (city), *ātman* (self), *bhakti* (devotion), *ens* (being), which all correspond to the state of sleeping and the area of the ontic.

The danger of the first dimension is sluggishness, of the second intellectualism. In the third, we have to recognize a certain sentimentality (the heart, feeling, all that has its place here but also its dangers). The veil of the first dimension is the will, which makes us look at everything under the aspect of good and evil—what to strive for and what to avoid. The veil of the second dimension is the truth, which we can see by means of reason and will. The veil of the third dimension is even more difficult to describe; it is connected here with the symbol of fire. Meister Eckhart calls it *velamen entis,* "the veil of being," of being at large.

Ens: I want to explain the problem we are dealing with here with an example from the history of religion: The historic misunderstanding between christianity and buddhism has its essential origin in the fact that from an *ātmavāda* position—from the viewpoint, that is, that there exists a firm substance, a firm central point of being, a "soul," in the person—one cannot understand the *anātmavādin* (the follower of the *anātman* teachings). Between *ātman* and *anātman* one cannot mediate on a doctrinal level, because the substantialization of being on the one hand, which makes the highest level of reality the ultimate of being, and on the other the conviction of an essential impossibility of substantialization of reality, which makes the "highest level of reality" *shūnyatā, nirvāna,* emptiness, are paradoxical views and cannot be united with a common denominator. But there are certain bridges in intellectual history, where both sides have not refused to enter dialogue. Likewise, in the christian (as well as in the jewish and islamic) tradition, one can find several authors who hold that being and reality are not identical.

Meister Eckhart connects this third veil with Romans VIII:18, which was mentioned above. Eckhart is talking here about the *gloria,* the *doxa,* the "glory"—that is, the splendor of the ultimate life. Revelation removes all covers. Revelation pulls away all that is covering up glory: the veil of the good, the veil of the true, and also the veil of being itself. This process occurs "in us," as Eckhart emphasizes in reference to the latin text of the biblical passage. Since "the nature of the soul is far from the kingdom of this world, the soul's nature resides in another world above the soul's capacity, above intellect and will. . . . But the nature of the soul is never intruded upon by creation, and by God only without any covers" (LW IV,11,2).

We are not dealing at this point with intellectual dogmas. We must understand what Meister Eckhart has said from his special point of view; this has been said also by many buddhist traditions in their larger contexts—each tradition in its own language—a part of indic tradition, and by some branches of mysticism at various times. It is basically the insight that reality cannot be broken up and that therefore a separate self-awareness does not represent the order of reality. Reduced to a simple formula, one might say in reference to this hindu version: *brahman* is so much pure consciousness that it is not even consciousness *of something. Brahman* is not even aware of itself; therefore, *brahman* does not know it is *brahman. Brahman* does not know *anything!* Īshvara, on the other hand, knows that it is *brahman*—and, knowing it, it is *brahman.*

Polis: Continuing our previous parallelism of words, one might say: "I am *ātman,* I am *polis,* I am *fire,* I am *bhakti." Bhakti* is devotion and love. *Polis* means city, tribe, community, political society. We are not talking about a community coming into existence as the result of high spiritual goals and ideals, but about the tribe, the natural community, which is natural because its members live in one another's neighborhood, because one knows the other, because they go into battle together and are, in a sense, blood-related. Telephones and television sets are only substitutes for real neighborly relations. I do not mean that in a racist sense but in a true, down-to-earth, bodily, political, communal sense, in contrast to some utopian communities. The human being not only lives in a community, not only belongs to a certain society; Man is community, is *polis.*

Concerning the western tradition of this symbol, one would completely misunderstand the greek *polis* if one regarded it as a purely technical thing, a democracy only formed for assessing the rules of people's behavior. A *polis* is a *mesocosm,* a field where micro- and macrocosm encounter each other. A *polis* cannot be imagined without its temples, its Gods, its vertical dimension. All these are part of it, as water is part of a swimming pool. Where else but in the *polis,* in political life, does one perfect the self, reaching one's contentment, allowing all the possibilities of one's personality to flourish? Where else is one deified, cured, saved? (Political life is in this sense, of course, more than a parliamentary dabbling with laws.) The fullness of the person becomes reality only in communion with the Gods, the neighbors, the things, the animals—with all creatures, that is, constituting a *polis*. Without all the above, a *polis*, a *civitas*, could never offer such fullness to the human being.

It was Augustine who destroyed this comprehensive meaning of *polis* in the christian tradition—primarily in order to help the people of his time rescue political life—by distinguishing between *civitas Dei* and *civitas terrena*, the city of God and the city of the world. Why? Augustine lived during a time when both greek and roman ideals were disintegrating. The natural community of the *polis* was practically destroyed. The majority of people could not reach the ideal of becoming perfected in the city, in the political life. The old Gods were banished, their sacred things defaced. During Augustine's time, followers of the old Gods were already persecuted. The christian God had been introduced by Constantine for a political reason—a fact we criticize all too easily, as terrible as its consequences may have been for later christianity. But the old political order of the Roman Empire, though in the midst of decay, was the only order imaginable at that time.

Augustine maintained the unity of heaven and Earth and wanted to rescue the unity of human life, which reached its perfection in the *polis*. But he knew well—as difficult as it may be to understand from our post-Enlightenment position—that it was an unrealizable dream of the human being to reach salvation in one single *polis*. There were too many slaves, women, children—too many people who did not take part in this perfecting process, in this deification process as it should have taken place in the *polis*. So Augustine opens a window and presents to people a divine city (not simply some vague heaven in which everyone believed anyway) by telling them: Since it is impossible for people to realize human life here and live it out, they have this city of God as a real *polis*, as another chance. This is a great thought as a pastoral theme, but historically speaking it is the beginning of a dichotomy of Heaven and Earth, one that has henceforth characterized christianity. Perhaps there is a possibility today of bringing about a reconciliation between the two poles. This is, in fact, one of the main duties christians have.

Atman: I *am* community. The person cannot realize one's life, realize one's existence, without being something other than this individual, singular ego. The person cannot simply be concerned with controlling one's body, decorating one's soul, and cultivating a good relationship with one Thou. The wealth of Man goes much further. I am not simply individual. This is what the word *ātman* indicates. This word cannot really be translated. The common equivalent "self" is just as enlightening as it is deceptive. The fact that I am *ātman* or, better, the fact that *ātman* is what I am too constitutes the discovery of the third dimension of being. However, this third dimension cannot be the discovery of reason. The *ātman* must reveal itself, because in it everything becomes unity. One should follow this *ātman* around and track it, since through it one recognizes things.

I would like to describe briefly the basic experience necessary for finding *ātman* by referring to today's scientific-technological world in which most of us live. The chinese people of the thirteenth century saw something similar with even greater clarity, and also the *upanishads* of the sixth century B.C. give us a hint of it. We, too, are beginning to feel its consequences: It is the theoretical impossibility of being conversant in all areas of knowledge. I cannot know everything. The more I know, the more I know that I do not know. Thus, an inflation of knowledge develops, which is just as bad as our population explosion. Literature today is so vast and complex that no one can read everything, not even in one's special field. I rely on excerpts from excerpts of a certain kind of literature. But how can I understand anything when trying to get to know *everything* (in a quantitative sense)? Can I do any more than simply understand this or that singular aspect? Then I begin to understand that even if I assumed that I could know everything, this knowledge will not give me true understanding.

Such was Heraclitus's complaint against the followers of Pythagoras. The indic tradition is also familiar with this problem:

Where there is such a thing as duality, there one sees the other; one smells the other; one tastes the other; one talks to the other; one listens to the other; one thinks of the other; one touches the other; one understands the other. But when everything has already become *ātman* to me, with what and with whom could one see; could one smell; could one taste; could one talk; could one listen; could one think; could one touch; could one understand? It is that by which one can understand the whole of reality: How can one understand this thing? It is not like this or that (*neti—neti*). It is incomprehensible because it cannot be comprehended; indestructible because it cannot be destroyed; independent because it cannot be tied down; it is free, cannot be upset, cannot be harmed: How could one understand the Understander?" (BU IV,5,15)

The proper question then is, "How can I understand what understands everything?" (BU II,4,14).

What is necessary here is a radical reversal of our civilization's direction: it is either geared toward the production of things (technocracy) or toward the perfection of subjects (humanism). Both are basic orientations, mutually exclusive in their goals. In our time, technocracy rules humanism. When gaining power is at stake, some can—but always only a minority!—be quite easily successful by means of technocracy. When it is a matter of dominating, changing (or destroying) this world, we are quick to act these days. But becoming personally fulfilled depends on completely different factors. Some people reach this goal, others do not. Yet this is the point: to attain personal fulfillment in life and personal participation in life's fullness. (I would call the *humanum* in the *quaternitas perfecta* "humanism," which does not denote the common anthropological image of Man, as I have explained already in *Humanismo y Cruz* [1963].) To say it in words of the christian tradition, we are dealing with *gloria, exousia,* and *doxa;* the glory, the splendor of what is real. What is life for? What is the one thing that makes us not only move but *be*?

We are dealing here with a basic orientation of communal, not individual, nature: Whether or not the individual is happy may be an individual question. But whether or not the priorities of our civilization are directed toward happiness or toward power only the community can determine. This is the third dimension, and here we are beginning to fathom already that in order for being to be, we have to let it be. We have to let being be in the double sense of the word. After all, we are discovering that the purity of being's self is tainted the moment my thought, my will, or my self gets involved.

Here the breach of Augustine's split becomes apparent: my salvation, my wholesome health—that is, my realization as a human being—no longer takes place in the realm of the here and now, of present existence, but in the kingdom of having-it-all-later in the *civitas Dei* (not *hominum*). Thereby one practically loses the validity of the request: "As in Heaven, so on Earth" (Matt. VI:10).

Fire and bhakti: At this point, the symbolism of fire, as viewed by many human traditions, is important. Fire devours, rages, and destroys. It turns things to ashes, which the wind scatters. Fire can only be fire as long as there is something to burn. It is fire because something is burned in it. By becoming fire, this something ceases to exist and makes fire possible. Fire feeds on what enables it to live. It is not like earth. In hinduism, *agni* is what destroys itself, what gives itself power to live, a power only realized when surrendering in self-sacrifice. In buddhism, *nirvāna* is, literally interpreted, the extinction of fire. When nothing is left of the candle, everything is burned and the flame ceases to exist by itself. After all, the flame is nothing but wax not yet become fire.

Christian tradition speaks of two books, the book of life (Holy Scripture, which the sages read and which requires a certain amount of preliminary knowledge) and the book of nature, which *everyone* can read. Augustine says that Holy Scripture is elitist, only directed to a few; the book of nature is for everyone, even—to translate it literally—for the "idiots" (*idiotes* literally means "laypersons," "common uneducated people"). In the former body of writings only the scholars read, but in the world and in nature even the uninitiated can read. Augustine says: "let God's page [that is, Holy Scripture] be a book to you so you will hear [one "hears" the book!]; let the whole world be a book to you so you will see." Augustine knew that, according to Paul, faith comes from hearing, but understanding from seeing. One can "hear" the book, perhaps glean some meaning for oneself from it; but one can "see" the world. The codices are made for the scholars, but the entire world is made for the ignorant. Bonaventure teaches that after the Fall "the book of the world died and was destroyed."[10] Through mercy, however, the things of the world were once again "as a book, in which the creating (*fabricatrix*) Trinity reflected, presented itself, and could become legible."[11]

Such is human wisdom grown out of traditions. It frees and removes us from the successes of our post-Enlightenment world, so that perhaps we will be enabled to gain a more universal human experience without remaining entangled in the hermeneutical net of the past three or four centuries. How can we dare to have fellowship with people—let alone having fellowship with the earth—when we are the *only* enlightened people in the world? We can never reach fellowship that way. We have to start learning to read all over again, this time not the books made of paper but the book of nature, which not only contains forests and rivers but a direct view of the world in which we live. Everyone can see—not only as an elitist "listener" of a book (which used to be read aloud in former days), but as a direct onlooker upon reality. This view has an ultimate, essential characteristic: Seeing is not reflecting on what has been seen, but it is simply a sighting, a viewing by which one is endowed. It is not solely like a perusing of a pretty picture album, which might help us remember but cannot replace memories with reality. In order to see, I must forget that I am seeing. Otherwise, I am only *thinking* that I see, *I am only imagining* that I see a beautiful landscape. True seeing is unmediated. And that is a universal analogy. It has nothing to do with some optical phenomenon; it is not thinking that I see; it is not enjoying what I see; it is simply seeing. That which is seen is something never seen before; not scrutinized, invisible—*ātman, polis,* fire, *bhakti. Bhakti* means here "love" and denotes the centrifugal power to come out of oneself and consume oneself, just as fire does.

If we cannot find meaning in these symbols and pictures, we might assume that a fundamental part of our humanness has been eliminated. In order to discover ourselves, to know ourselves in the depth of humanness given to us, we must truly live. This insight is expressed by the three dimensions discussed, the first triad of the *quaternitas perfecta.* Man is Man only when humanly living.

Fourth Center: Air and Spirit

In the 1930s, during a campaign of the Non-Cooperation Movement in Bihar, North India, Gandhi met a former classmate he had not seen in many years. The latter walked up to Gandhi to greet him. He did not wear handmade clothes, which was the sign of Gandhi's

movement for independence, but "english" clothes. The two sur-
veyed each other and recognized the situation very quickly. The
friend explained: "I have to live somehow! Five children, mother-in-
law. . . ." Gandhi replied, "I don't see the necessity." And he walked
off with his people. Either—or. It is hard having to feed many hungry
mouths. The man was working for the government service; and if
they saw him associating with those half-naked fellows, he would lose
his job. He had to make money, do good, provide for his family. . . .
Gandhi had other priorities and walked off.

This is an illustration of the spiritual life. One risks everything: "If
your hand or foot gives you trouble, chop it off and throw it away
from you" (Matt. XVIII:8); "Whoever wants to save one's life, will
lose it" (Matt. XVI:25). Just as uncompromising is Shankara's
Vivekachūdāmani (21,79,164,299,508, and many other passages).
We either accept the spiritual life with all our heart by thrusting
ourselves into it with intensity and passion or we view it only as a new
luxury article to be consumed. Everyone will have to experience this
dilemma at least once in life. Life is in our hands. We forge our
destiny ourselves, although external forces may influence us and play
their part. Life does not exclude coincidence or providence. As a
writer, I may have to wait for inspiration coming from the outside:
"The spirit blows where it wills" (John III:8). But if the Holy Spirit
does not find me with pen in hand, inspiration will pass me by and
remain useless.

The fourth dimension is air (breath, spirit), *kosmos* (*ākāsha*,
ether, the open space), *brahman*, *tūshnīm* (being silent), *nihil* (nothing, emptiness), *turīya* (the "fourth" [state], which transcends waking, dreaming, and sleeping), the realm of the mystical. One cannot
see this one, only guess it; sometimes it even rips apart trees,
carrying with it a mighty force. There is no veil here because there is
nothing to hide. There is nothing to hide, no *velamen,* because there
is simply nothing: it is nothing and does not say anything.

We have an innate experience that can help us describe this
dimension. It is the experience of *freedom*—not the concept of
freedom itself or the idea, but the experience. Certainly freedom
does not mean here being able to choose at the supermarket between
two kinds of tea. When life consists only of choosing between things

given, we do not really live. We only live when risking this life over and over, when allowing life to live.

If we cannot succeed doing so in a natural way, the bold ones in society and the young generation will teach us in their own ways that life wants to be lived by means of risking it. But there are also mad drivers, drug addicts, people who are doing something that gives them at least the impression of living because they put their lives at stake. When many sensitive people of a society can experience life only by means of such dreadful things, it is proof we are not living life at all because of fear, the need for reassurance, and protection. I consider those activities a perversion but not a negation of life. If we are not, in both word and deed and by our convictions, truly lived by life itself, if we are only experimenting with what is safe and pleasant and does not appear dangerous, then we are not living. A life not lived takes vengeance through death. Life wants to live, but repressed life seeks death. The tragic events of our century, which—out of the midst of a modern civilization of order and security—have led to modern warfare, should be a warning to us.

The experience of life and the experience of our actual situation belong together—and that even in the area of knowledge. This view contradicts, of course, Descartes' philosophy, whose concern for certainty has enticed us, with our consent, into having a certainty and security complex. Bonaventure, a contemporary of Thomas Aquinas, says in amazingly severe words: "Concerning the theory that some kind of science is all the more valuable (noble), the greater its certainty, one will have to say that this science does not contain any truth."[12] And the ingenuous Augustine formulated an earlier version of the Cartesian *cogito ergo sum: Si enim fallor, sum:* "Even if [I am] mistaken, I [still] am" (*De civitate Dei* XI, 26).

Nihil: We have to probe yet deeper. True experience of life carries with it the experience of contingency, the touching (*tangere*) upon the nothing. "If someone upon seeing God knew what he saw, he has not truly seen God," Dionysius Areopagita says.[13] A text of shivaism from Kashmir says: "The biggest secret is that there is no secret."[14] Evagrius Ponticus says: "Blessed is the one who has reached infinite ignorance."[15] Ignorance, *agnosia, ignorantia*—yet it needs be infinite!

But I am also this: Brahman, which does not even know it is *brahman;* ether; the empty space (which has little to do with the empty space of science); the wind; breath. It shows that, when limiting the ego to our small person, to the community, or to our social relationships, wc have only little regard for ourselves. What we need most is to be convinced of our dignity. "Above all respect thyself," say the Pythagorean Golden Verses (8).[16] We are lacking experience of our own infinity; we do not have enough self-confidence; we lack the awareness that we are not just a particle in the universe—that would be ridiculous if viewing the universe only in terms of quantity. No, we are a mirror of all of reality (to use an old metaphor). It is a very special mirror, where reality shines in such a way that the differences disappear. Nothing can be seen in it except what antiquity already called, the microcosm. Yet at the same time this mirror contains also the entire macrocosm. Both microcosm and macrocosm belong essentially together.

Silence: At this point, the word "contemplation" is appropriate. It has very little to do with such words as "deliberation," "reflection," or "theory." Contemplation is not a synthesis of *action* and *theôria,* of practice and theory, but it is the very ground where both practice and theory originate. Contemplation has both an intellectual and a practical aspect; thinking leads to a certain clarity, practice to a certain change of affairs. Contemplation is not a mixture of both; nor is it a synthesis; but it is this basic attitude where both knowledge and action have not yet been separated. The ancients used to say: *Operari sequitur esse* (action follows being). Later, people viewed it the other way around: *Esse sequitur operari.* Though both action and knowledge may be distinguished as different ideas, we only *are* when both action and knowledge are not separated. This is certainly the true, human experience.[17] Contemplative life is neither pure meditation nor pure action; instead, it is the action upon which one reflects and the meditation upon which one acts, the undivided life. Its name is wisdom.

We have to emphasize here that Man is not an isolated being on whom external relationships have been heaped as a supplement. These relationships would then be only circumstantial. Instead, Man

61

is constituted by the totality of those relationships which form, by nature, Man as a whole. One might stress again that the anthropological thought of today's dominant civilization is much too narrow in defining the human being. When animals are simply viewed as machines, as the west has practically done following Descartes, then the human being becomes in the modern view a "rational machine" following Aristotle's definition of Man as *animal rationale*. Such a view is of very little use for our *quaternitas*.

Here lies the existential core of our discussion: the correlation between *karman, jñāna,* and *bhakti* (action, understanding, and love) is complete; nothing is missing. Therefore, one might choose the word *tûshnîm*, quietude, silence, calm, for the fourth dimension in order to round up the *quaternitas*. Other traditions have chosen, for example, *sigê, silentium, sosiego, Abgeschiedenheit*. This kind of quietude does not refer to a quietude of thought, which would be *yoga;* not to a quietude of action, which would not be human; not to a quietude of the heart, which could be fatal.

Instead, this silence is something the old chinese called *wu wei;* Chuang-tzu describes it as an unintentionality that is the necessary prerequisite for every authentic action: "The not-acting is the law of the sage" (XIII,3). The Tao-te king says: "The sage is effective without acting, teaches without talking" (2)—mainly, because this not-doing is also a part of Man. Christian mariologists would call it "the fullness of grace"—as Mary heard from the angel (Luke I:28). In many, the elements of nature, culture, and grace are in full harmony and union. There is nothing artificial or stilted added here. Nevertheless, it is not mere passivity, not quietism, because it is part of Man's dignity of being commissioned to bring the universe to perfection. Perhaps one could call it the cosmic rhythm that enters and penetrates us and is transformed by us at the same time that we adapt to it. The rhythm of being is not predetermined; harmony is creative and, at the same time, has to be created.

The Mystical: If the first center comprises the area of the moral, the second the psychological, and the third the ontic, we have to speak here of the mysticism. But one must be careful with the word "mystical," because there is danger of turning it, first, into "mist" (fog) and then into "schism" (split). That would not be a good thing, yet this danger cannot be avoided. The highest and most noble things in this world are primarily those that can have the worst consequences and can turn sour. True mysticism, however, is part of this harmonious not-knowing, of this inner peace, of this unquenchable joy that so easily turns into cynicism, indifference, inhumanness, and other things.

What could the word "mystical" mean? One might employ here the analogy of the "third eye." Since Plato, greek tradition says that the sum total of reality can be known by means of the empirical, through the five senses of seeing, touching, tasting, smelling, hearing. The *aisthêsis*—which really means "sensuousness"—is a human feature and is indispensable for all spiritual practices. If it is overlooked, it will have negative consequences. Sensuousness is not only essentially human; it is also an essential ingredient of reality. In sensuousness, in the aesthetic, beauty resides. *Kosmos* means both jewel and world. The greek orthodox tradition of christianity, which is close to pre-christian philosophy, says that the first attribute of God is beauty.

If one loses sensuousness, one is lost. But one has to penetrate sensuousness—not simply supplement it—by the intellect, by the *nous,* by the rational, by reasoning, by our intellectual consciousness, which cannot be separated from sensuousness. If this penetration is successful, we will be able to develop our sensuousness, our will, and our reasoning. Man is a sensuous but also a rational being. We must not neglect the intellectual dimension of the person; if we were to do away with it, we no longer would be human beings. Reason has its rights, and it would be suicidal to contest them.

Nevertheless, it appears that in some cultures the image of Man and the concept of reality have been reduced to these two dimensions. This is the great danger inherent in all exclusively technocratic civilizations. People of all times, even those of cultures thinking highly dualistically, remind us that there is still a third eye which opens up to us a third facet of reality. Along with Plato, one might call the first dimension *ta aisthêta,* the second *ta noêta,* and the third *ta mystika:* the mystical.

We have a third "organ" that helps us get in touch with reality just as the other sense organs do. The senses correspond to the material and space-time dimensions of reality. The intellect, the *nous,* corresponds to the intellectual dimension of reality, which is just as real as the physical. We say, for example, "justice" and "truth," whereby a certain meaning is involved, a creative, reality-creating force. But there is still this third, additional sense indicative of an otherwise invisible dimension of reality. That is the mystical, the unpronounceable, which cannot be named so that, when still needing a word for it, one might call it "nothing" or "the nothing."

The relationship of this third dimension to the second is analogous to the relationship between the third and the first. The person cannot have purely sense-related perception; it is always somehow related to the intellect or to consciousness. In a similar fashion, one cannot have intellectual perception without the presence of the third dimension. This third dimension comes into play in such a way that it allows us to "sense" intellectual insight; to "see" that there "is more" than the intellect can convey to us. By means of the intellect the person fathoms that reality, even the smallest particle of being, is of infinite depth. Likewise, one fathoms by means of the intellect that reality might also be different from the presumed. This means that both infinity and freedom are two basic human experiences which presuppose reason yet transcend reason at the same time.

Our three "organs," windows, sense potentials for reality, are inseparably connected. When I am thinking, my brain is involved. When I am sensing, my intellectual awareness is also involved. Similarly, this third "organ" is always present. Reality cannot be reduced to two dimensions. It is the role of the third "organ" to deepen the two others. Its nature is to penetrate them in such a way that the third organ itself remains invisible, unpronounceable, undetected. Whenever people attempted to turn mysticism into a special field, severed from other dimensions of life, mysticism earned a bad reputation, and justly so.

The assumption of being able to speak of this third dimension without including the other two, is contradictory. As soon as one imagines that this third eye, this revelation of the highest, this special place of the heart could remain single and independent from the senses and intellect, the corruption so often connected with the word religion begins. Only by opening up to the sense-related, the material, and to the intellectual dimensions of reality do we experience that these alone are not sufficient. Thereby, either slowly or quickly, we realize the third dimension. But at the same time we cannot dispute the fact that especially those peoples of the world who call themselves "developed," are in general spiritually underdeveloped and suffering from a cultural atrophy of their third organ.

Teresa of Avila was cured of this pride in the mystical life during her first years in the convent. A new mother superior was to be elected—in those days there still existed a kind of democracy in the convents. In her state of spiritual rapture, Teresa heard a supernatural voice, which assured her that it was the will of God for her to become mother superior. So she was smiling to herself about all the others, the little politicians, who even in convents were busy working and staging an "election campaign" of sorts. Then the election came, and Teresa did not win. Crestfallen, she walked up to the crucifix and complained over the misfortune that had struck in spite of her good connections to the divine. Teresa was smart enough not to expect a special kind of revelation. Nevertheless, she could hear all of a sudden very clearly the answer amidst her tears: "Well, Teresa, *I* certainly wanted you to become mother superior, *but the nuns did not!*" A mysticism that went against the will of the nuns would have been impossible. God wanted one thing, but the nuns did not. Mysticism alone will not do.

The mystical without the intellectual is a ghost. The mystical without the sensuous is nonhuman. But likewise, the sensuous without the intellectual and the mystical is crippled and banal. Thoughts by themselves, without the magma from which they emerge, and which enables understanding, are simply arms of intellectual violence. The three are essentially one.

But there is one difference: The sensuous can be cultivated. One needs discipline and even asceticism for that. The intellectual can also be cultivated, though this discipline is much more refined. Although the will cannot be commanded—otherwise it would not be the will—yet it does not simply depend on itself alone. Therefore, freedom is more than a matter of the will. One has to cultivate the will in a very gentle manner. The intellect cannot be forced, but it can be trained. True training is not military training.

In the case of the mystical, things are even more subtle: again, one *has to* cultivate it. In contrast to the sensuous and the intellectual, one *cannot* either force it or train it; it is not a matter of training nor of the will. It is primarily the craving for *nirvāna* that is the great obstacle to reaching *nirvāna*. The will for holiness leads to hypocrisy and pride. The desire to become a spiritual personality or a spiritual person in order to have a little more peace, a little less sorrow, a better mood, or whatever, is exactly what leads to frustration. This urge is ultimately responsible for the epidemic of depression in our modern era. Depression simply means that there exists some pressure against another "pressure." Depression is an illness of the will: I aim high, and then something interferes by opposing my will—and I feel frustrated.

The mystical cannot be trained or cultivated; however, it can be loved. We are simply at its beckoning. One cannot love on command. Love is creative, real, without a why (*sunder Warumbe* [Eckhart]). Only purity of the heart puts us in a position where this third dimension of the quiet, of the invisible, complements the other two. That is all. It means that the "will as primordial being" does not have the final say. The way to spirituality is ultimately not a way. Still, we cannot be satisfied by mere faith, simply because we have to use also the intellect and the senses. We cannot rely on the fact that everything is grace, a divine gift that we simply receive. Though everything is grace, the process will have to start over and over again—and never without us. As long as we live, we will never see the end of this process. The new innocence is an innocence that perpetually renews itself.

Kosmos: At this point, we must say something about freedom: Freedom has very little to do with freedom of choice. Choosing only means deciding—dividing, that is, between "A" and "B"—thus making a cut through reality. Freedom cannot result in separation. Solomon knew that when pronouncing his famous verdict. There are no half children; the mother will not allow the child to be torn in half, even if the judge may not place it in her custody (1 Kings III:16–28). One says that "choosing is losing," losing sleep over one's decision or losing the part not chosen. But this kind of losing, or suffering, is not what freedom means.

How do I experience being free? What do I experience in being free? First, I have to experience that I am free from fear; that is the prerequisite: to be free from the fear of life, of death, of success, of failure, of love, of disdain, of suffering, of the truth, of myself. Fear has to disappear in all its stages. It is absent not because there are no longer any frightening objects around—there is also fear of the nothing—but because the subject which should have fear is no longer present. It is not true that there are no longer any ghosts, any threatening power figures, or whatever; instead, my core, which is supposed to hold fear, no longer exists.

It is understandable that complete absence of fear is not possible as long as the person is not free, as long as there is still the *ego*. As long as the *ego* exists, fear may even be beneficial. Without a certain amount of fear, human life would turn into chaos. Hence, we do not mean that every kind of fear is despicable; we are simply saying that every kind of fear stifles freedom.

Second, when I am free of fear and, in this sense, free of inhibitions, then I am detached from all kinds of limitations. I do not mean by that the borderlines or parameters that are part of my personal nature. These simply determine me, thereby enabling me to embrace reality. (This may be said against every kind of individualism which misunderstands freedom as limitlessness.) Instead, freedom is a much deeper dimension of existence, one that ultimately cannot limit what I do and am. Freedom in this sense is not a question of my parents' and grandparents' chromosomes, of culture and language, of social relationships and other circumstances. Instead, freedom is where I am experiencing, metaphysically speaking, nothingness (which is an experience without content, an experience of nothing in particular). This experience cannot be described; one can only radiate it. It symbolizes the fact that my life is not done living and that the life of this life is not dependent on highway directions, business orders, or some other externals. Instead it is dependent on *nothing*. As a result of such an experience, I will certainly not commit suicide; that would be proof of my imprisonment, of my attachment to externals of which I want to rid myself. Freedom does not need to be set free.

Freedom is the experience of infinity, of the fact that no one else has ever been what I am. At its beginning is the experience of my uniqueness. There is something inside me that makes *me* capable of forgetting, that makes *me* perhaps envious of things, goods, and people which or whom *I* would rather enjoy, *I* would rather have. It is something inside me that I try covering up with all this envy, this greed or this love. And this something is unique, untransferable. And this I is, speaking in a paradox, *entrusted to me*. It is I who am that central point of reality which is, in this particular instance, determined by no one else but me. The seriousness of this life, the experience of this freedom consists in the fact that something is entrusted to me which is irreplaceable, and this something is I. The whole universe exists, but I exist too with the constant possibility of not being—when the me takes hold of the I.

What we are talking about could be best illustrated by the now-unpopular belief in hell. The seriousness of the belief in hell is the experience, on the one hand, that there is something inside me which wants to grow and be but which, on the other, can be lost in a sort of abortion process. I am not a spare part which can be exchanged. If I do not enact what I am, no one else will. Here no one else can help me out, no one can replace me, since it is not a matter of doing a certain job, of having a certain function. It is a matter of being, not having. The point is that something within me is ultimate and cannot be reversed. Job speaks of the path that cannot be retraced (Job XVI:22). Such is the experience of freedom, the highest good of the human being.

Thomas Aquinas says: "Sinners, as far as they are sinners, do not exist" (*Summa Theologiae* I,q.20,a.2,ad.4). "Inquantum vero peccatores sunt, non sunt, sed ab esse deficiunt." Something that could have been born into eternal life has not been born. There will be forever a hole in its place. It is not a matter of five minutes or some limited amount of time; there will not be any I ever. I have lost my I, my reality. That is hell. Thus, we understand the christian tradition of the poet Dante: "The divine power made me, the highest wisdom, and the primal love" (*Inferno* III, 5–6):

> Giustizia mosse il mio alto fattore:
> fecemi la divina potestate,
> la somma sapïenza e'l primo amore.

Hell is the work of divine justice.

It means I am unique, irreplaceable, not a replica of some other model. It also means that I should not imitate anyone else. That does not imply that I am particularly important or will enjoy extended longevity in the cosmos, which may be suggested by the idea of hell. I once comforted an anguished lady concerning her fear of hell and told her that this eternity, which is hell, will not even last a minute. Eternity has no duration.

The way to find spirituality is not a way, as Abhinavagupta (*upayā-nupaya*) and also John of the Cross state: "At the peak of the mountain there is no path . . . at the peak of the mountain: nothing." It is a paradox: an introduction to true spirituality is to experience a reality that has not been created yet, which is not dependent on a ready-made image of Man or an a priori worldview; rather, it is the experience of a reality just now newly created by us. Since there is no way or path, we do not have the fear of losing it, of becoming lost. The point is to awaken in us a genuine vitality, which I have tried to suggest above. Only when arriving at this in-depth level where we are truly helpless, where central reality opens up to us in form of the experience of grace or of one's inner condition, where the I is nothing more than a receiver; only then will we, paradoxically, experience the freedom that sets us free from every kind of fear and the feeling of self-sufficiency. Then we will experience the uniqueness of our lives, which mirrors, each individually, the entire universe.

This is the mystery of Man, a *quaternitas* which is, on the one hand, reflected in each one of us, and which, on the other hand, allows us by means of its mirror effect to remain ourselves.

The following table illustrates what has been said:

I	II	III	IV
Earth	Water	Fire	Air
sōma	*psychē*	*polis*	*kosmos*
jîva	*aham*	*âtman*	*brahman*
karman	*jñâna*	*bhakti*	*tûshnîm*
bonum	*verum*	*ens*	*nihil*
Waking	Dreaming	Sleeping	Being Silent
the Moral	the Psycho-logical	the Ontic	the Mystical

Questions and Answers on the "Perfect Fourfoldness"

The Bible says that the Spirit blows where it wills (John III:8). From that follows that the Spirit is not at the person's disposal; hence, everything the person can understand remains veiled and incomplete. Further, Paul says: "Now we look into a mirror and only see dimly, then we will see face to face" (I Cor. XIII:12). How, then, can you speak of tearing apart the three veils? How can this kind of knowledge about the religious paths, the knowledge of the "quaternitas perfecta," be free from these veils that ultimately conceal the proper path? The statement from John XIV:6, "I am the way, the truth, and the life," seems to indicate that the path is veiled. How would you look at a person who believes in this statement?

The fact that we *merely believe* in a statement does not make us christians. If I believe that Jesus has risen yet do not take part in this resurrection process, my faith will only be theoretical. We are "children of God, being children of the resurrection," said Christ (Luke XX:36). The mysteries concerning Christ are also our mysteries. If we do not participate in them, we will not enjoy their fruit. Faith is not a thought process, not a mere assumption of facts. Instead, faith denotes the existential participation in the fate of Jesus Christ, in his experience and reality. If he has risen, then I have risen also—or I am on my way there (cf. Rom. VI:8). If he is the truth, then I will be it also by means of identifying with him (cf. John VI:58; Phil. I:21; II Cor. V:15; etc.).

A christian especially can say and find strength in that, since Jesus shows us that it may be true. The mysteries of Jesus' death and resurrection are not exceptions only in case of Jesus. He dies so that *we* may have life. He rose so that *we* may rise. He is truth so that *we* may say what he said. Otherwise, we only pride ourselves in having a great leader. That is not a faith that saves. Faith is always personal participation, never magic. In responding to the theological questions about faith, I would have to refer to my other writings. I only want to say in a philosophical manner that the existential statement "I *am* the truth" is not identical with the purely objective statement "Christ *is* the truth," because in the latter case, the subject is no longer Christ but my understanding of him. The symbol of the path is chosen properly: the veils are (only) around for the journey. But revelation means the unveiling of each of these veils (faith is *inchoatio vitae aeternae* [the beginning of life eternal]).

How does what you have said about the "quaternitas perfecta" relate to the christian doctrine of the Trinity? Does the Trinity not emphasize clearly that God is absolute and thus also christianity as a religion? Does the upshot of your statements not bypass the clear christian doctrines as they describe the relationship, for example, of the Father to the Son and the Spirit; of God to the person and the world? Can the Trinity be converted into a kind of creation theology? Are you not interpreting everything too much in light of anthropological categories? Or could we speak of some sort of ecumenical trinitarian doctrine, which declares these clear christian doctrines as narrow and wishes to transcend them?

Indeed, what we are saying here has far-reaching consequences, which cannot be taken lightly. Perhaps I may confess here to being an orthodox, in contrast to a heterodox or a microdox, christian who enjoys his freedom primarily because of Christ's doings (see Gal. V:1, 13; Rom. VIII:21; II Cor. III:17; etc.).

In this book I have dealt solely with anthropology, having dealt with theology in others. I do not consider theology and anthropology identical, though both belong together. Any teaching about God is always anthropology because it also involves how the *anthrôpos* accepts, understands, and practices theology. Indeed, I am so convinced of the central importance of the Trinity that it is the reason I am not calling myself a monotheist—without being a tritheist. I simply want to emphasize one aspect: the Trinity is not a monopoly of God. All of reality is trinitarian.

In today's theology there is talk of an "immanent Trinity," which is the inner relationships of the divine persons, Father, Son, and Holy Spirit. But there is also a theology of an "economic Trinity"— and that is what the first theological tradition sets forth, beginning with the church fathers. Economy is the saving action of God in creation. An economic Trinity means that everything created by God reflects the image of the trinitarian God and that the entire Trinity participates in the process of creation. It is a classical theological model. In the words of Thomas Aquinas: *Unus idemque actus quo Pater generat Filium creat mundum* ("The act of the Father's begetting the Son [the intratrinitarian act] and the Father's creating the world is one and the same").[18]

I can still go a step farther and speak, besides the immanent and the economic Trinity, of the *radical Trinity.* The latter means that all of reality is trinitarian in the sense that our referring to "God" or "Man" will always remain merely abstract. I cannot speak of God without remembering what God has done. God's nature and God's doing are inseparable. Therefore, that which God has done is part of God's nature. God, Man, and the World are merely three abstractions. There is no God without Man, no Man without World, no World without God. The three are all one when we speak existentially and in correspondence with reality. All that is real is related to God, to Man, and to Kosmos. There is nothing that is not related to Matter, Man, or God. Ultimately, these will be our categories. Therefore, the divine is everywhere, as is also the material and the human.

A true view of reality consists of discovering the divine, the material, and the human in every being and in every small particle. I call it the *cosmotheandric* or the *theanthropocosmic insight.* Hence, the Trinity becomes the starting point for the ecumenical movement, the encounter and mutual enrichment of the differing religious traditions.

To reply briefly to the question on creation, I think I am entitled to say as a christian that the beginning of the creation narrative (Gen. I:1) has to be interpreted through John I:3: "And everything has come into being through him [the Christ]."

Does this mean that the mystical three veils need to be interpreted not only in light of the doctrine concerning Jesus but also in light of the entire christian doctrinal system?

"Do not store away treasures where moths, worms, or thieves can do harm," the Sermon on the Mount says (Matt. VI:19).

In summary: The ultimate dignity of our lives is wisdom, and it lives only where no mind, no intellect, and no will can harm it. Anything that can be forgotten, any compilation of information, is certainly not wisdom. Anything that, by means of the intellect, can be mastered, comprehended, tackled, or controlled is not wisdom. Not without reason people of old distinguished between understanding or knowledge and wisdom (for example, Isa. XI:3). Wisdom is not only for the smart. Anything that can become the object of the will cannot possibly contain wisdom. Wisdom is not a matter of the will; it is not an object that can be manipulated by our will. It is for a good and simultaneously ironic reason that wisdom is often portrayed as a lady!

In the Gospel of Matthew it is written: "Where our heart is, there our treasure will be also" (Matt. VI:21). Wisdom will not live in us if our treasure is history, with all that could be lost; knowledge, with all that could be learned; or the good, with all that could be desired and collected. Wisdom is not present where something can be devoured or stolen by moth, worm, or thief. In fact, wisdom's nature is such that even all our spiritual powers cannot cause it any harm.

For that reason, only wisdom understands and accomplishes what is written also: "Do not worry about tomorrow!" (Matt. VI:34). With reason alone one cannot justify this injunction. In fact, reason would even consider the injunction irresponsible, and those who feel that way had better not free themselves of tomorrow's worries!

I could offer a dialectic answer but that would not make for a wise answer. I can only attest to the fact that the injunction is neither irrational nor intended to be thus. One had better be both dove and serpent at the same time! Whoever has eyes to see and ears to hear may touch upon and taste the *sapida scientia,* this wise (tasty) experience.

What do you mean by "polis" in your discussion of the "quaternitas perfecta"?

I have inserted the term *polis* as I have explored it in my french book, *Le métapolitique.* I refer to the metapolitical though some people may believe that it does not exist.

The problem is to define *ātman. Atman* does not exactly mean "self"; this is only a makeshift translation. *Atman* is the center of the kind of reality, both immanent and transcendent at the same time, that symbolizes the self-perfecting of the human being. This process is possible only in the *polis,* in this cosmic yet primarily human community where even mundane work has its place and is not downgraded. The point is this *ātman* as it is present in all of us. It does not concentrate merely on the tip of the soul and on human life alone, but it penetrates everything. Therefore, the symbol of this third dimension is fire; the human entry gate is not the intellect, but love, surrender, and so forth.

In your discussion of the "quaternitas" you did not mention the eros. Is it perhaps related to "bhakti" or to "sensuousness" or to both?

I did not explicitly mention eros because it is today so popular that it has become almost a triviality. Eros is, indeed, *bhakti;* it pervades everything. Sensuousness is eros also (although the word eros would have to be explained in this connection more closely). I do not exclude eros. In describing the notion of *bhakti* in its roots and development, the word eros plays an important role; however, it makes little sense to link everything, in an obsessive way, with eros.

We always exist in concrete situations. It is truest to life and most fitting to respond to what is most dominant and prevailing in a situation. A dominican monk once told me, "If you want to preach well, invent an enemy for yourself!" Knowing *against whom* to argue, you will have power. Just imagine how difficult it is when there is no opponent! That is the case here also; I did not feel the need to blast against the anti-eros. But you are right: if sensuousness is oppressed by christianity, if we have been spiritually castrated, it makes sense that we should defend eros imagery, sexual freedom, liberation, and all that. But other people might fear that by concentrating on eros we may not help in regaining a healthy attitude. Eros, like breathing, recovers its normal place the moment we remove repressions, so natural it is. We need liberation from constraints, but since this discussion deals with a different kind of liberation, I did not spend much time on something I almost took for granted.

Eros is important. The kind of inhibition, oppression, and repression that is rampant in protestant and roman catholic education is truly horrid and fatal, and one must fight it. But sometimes it may be best to engage in a passive battle by not taking everything so seriously. We should not abandon eros when trying to overcome anti-eros.

We have talked about taking away from children the originality that all of us want to gain back at one point. What is the function of parents in the development of their children so they can be spared the spiritual hardening we discussed? I see three possibilities. The first would be to raise the child in a religious environment. The second would be to preserve what is original in the child so that he or she will avoid the dilemma we adults are facing today. The third would involve both. Should parents not also be careful not to influence the child's development too much?

I would opt for the third suggestion. Here is a little story related to it:

A woman in Italy asked me to prepare her child for first communion. She was very concerned that the child receive the best instruction possible. I was to infiltrate the child with the liberating ideas of christianity. I told her: "I did not give up having children of my own so I could instruct other people's children. But if you like, I will teach you. Then you can tell the child yourself." She replied that she herself did not believe in God. "But your child is supposed to believe?" I asked. "I will give *you* first-communion instruction, if you like, but not the child."

Parents are indispensable. The child knows it, although it undertakes certain independent actions. That is not only culture but also nature. Parents cannot extricate themselves from this responsibility. I admit that parents have been, so far, much too forceful, too authoritarian, and primarily too possessive. The result is that the younger generation is saying "we have had enough" and wants to undo these fetters. It is certainly not the responsibility of parents to keep their children captives from a certain age on. On the other hand, the connection between parents and child is not solely determined by chromosomes. Therefore, communication between parents and child should also be marked by feedback and emulation or, to say it more traditionally, by parents setting an example. Here it is particularly important that we create this influence through our very existence: one cannot talk to one's spouse *one way* and to one's child *another*. One has to stay consistent. Other than this, there are no formulas.

III. Philosophy as Life-style

No word be without sound and body—
"Sino con la presencia y la figura."[1]

I cannot write about myself. First and foremost, I am not able to do so. I do not even have my own language. Second, I am all too aware that if I were to try, in spite of it, my self about which I would write would no longer be the self I am. After all, I am subject, not object. Third, writing about aspirations and resolutions resembles the activity of making plans. Reading about these might be interesting to friends and people with whom I have a personal relationship. But the interest stops right there in this personal frame of reference.

Yet I am still writing. I am not writing about myself; instead, my self is writing. All I am writing is, at least to a degree, a part of my self. Everything is somewhat autobiographical. I am using in my writing only words whose meaning I myself have grasped. It is this self of mine that I am writing about, and I am writing as one speaking.

I am especially careful to allow the *word* to speak, to allow language to develop its true self. The self, which *also* lives in the language (though it is different from the *ego*), speaks *on its own* and reveals its *self* when saying what *it* has to say. Thereby, this self does not pour out its heart; furthermore, the process of something becoming language does not happen automatically. Instead, the self needs me as a necessary mediator. I become an active element in this unveiling, and much depends on my transparency—in addition to my attention, among other things.

I remember an ideal I used to have: each paragraph I wrote, possibly each sentence, was to reflect my whole life and be an expression of my character. One was to be able to recognize my life in a single sentence of mine just as one could reconstruct the complete skeleton of a prehistoric animal by means of a single bone. I was concerned here with the symbolic interrelatedness of all living things. One single word, the *logos,* expressed the entire universe. Each of my words was to be similarly a symbol of my entire life. The interconnections of this symbol were not of mathematical (or merely coherent) but of vital nature.

Why am I writing? About that I would like to cite a fragment from notes I made years ago, long before others had asked me this question: *Why am I writing?* I am not simply writing in order to express myself, in order to articulate my thoughts, in order to grasp them better or to clarify them further. That is so, since all the above relate to the level of tools, yet tools for what purpose?

Well, instead of "living life having fun" or wanting "to do good" among certain people, I have a more challenging purpose, directed toward finishing some of my writings. Although it is clear that I am writing at the moment in order to turn in a manuscript I was asked for, it is certainly not my ultimate motivator.

I am not simply writing in order to transmit information or to provide communication. That would still be a means and not an end. Surely this way other people would be able to absorb my ideas. But for what purpose? What is ultimately the purpose of conveying a good idea? I have one and pass it on to another person. Now we two have it. That does not change the world. Or do I write to change the world? Are we still talking about a messianic calling?

If it is true that public ideas can change the world, and if I certainly want to change the world during my life, I should spend my time with mass media, with propaganda. Or perhaps I should dedicate my life to the movie and television industries. To say it directly, in order to change the world, to save the universe, as both buddhists and christians might say, one does not necessarily need to transform the majority opinion.

But are numbers a mere illusion? Two people with good ideas are not enough, but two million might be? Such is the myth of democracy. More than three billion people want disarmament, but nothing happens. It is likely that the majority of the world's population wants disarmament, and still we do not have it. It depends neither on the nature of the ideas nor on numbers.

Why, then, am I taking on the hard discipline of writing? Should I perhaps not ask the question why and instead simply follow my inclination? That might be the thing to do; for decades I have been doing it that way, not asking for a why. But once the why pops up, I cannot, I should not, repress it.

If I were to reply simply that I was writing because it is a part of my life, then that would be true, yet not enough. Why, then, am I directing my life this way and not that?

I am not writing in order to influence people, not even in order to cultivate an art—though that might be getting closer to the truth. Writing, to me, is meditation—that is, medicine—and also moderation, order for this world.[2] Writing, to me, is intellectual life, and that in turn is spiritual existence. The climax of life is, in my opinion, to participate in the life of the universe, in both the cosmic and divine symphonies to which even we mortals are invited. It is not only a matter of living but also of letting life be—this life, offered to us as a gift so that we may sustain and deepen it. Therefore, writing is a religious undertaking to me. By "religion" I mean the activity by which we human beings are saving, liberating, participating in, beautifying, and perfecting the universe. We are doing so by means of saving, liberating, perfecting the microcosms that we ourselves are—or by means of deifying these microcosms, some might say.

Writing allows and almost forces me to ponder deeply the mystery of reality. It certainly involves thinking, contemplation. But at the same time, writing means that I have to add form, shape, beauty, expression, revelation to this mystery of reality. Writing is *nāma-rūpa* and equally *ātman;* it is *morphê* in both essence and form. Writing presupposes thinking but also shaping and carving out thoughts; cleaning them, clothing them with colors, smells, and forms, even strengthening and putting them to action. It is an incarnation process where the "word becomes flesh." (That is what my notes from more than a quarter of a century ago are saying.)

I have been asked what I have to say concerning the "relationship of my personal life to my professional occupation." The first difficulty in answering this question is the fact that I do not see any sense in separating what is commonly called "personal life" and "professional occupation." I cannot separate my personal life from my occupation, which is, likewise, personal. Not without reason am I distinguishing between work and labor, "doing" in terms of creative activities, and "laboring" in order to make a living.

Doing is the activity of my being, the actualization of my potentials in order to make this world with its people—including myself—a better place. The religious language of Abraham's time terms it "calling." Doing in this sense entails the actualization of what I have been called to do, which eventually will lead to the fulfillment of my existence. Laboring, on the other hand, entails offering one's abilities to someone or to something in exchange for a previously arranged monetary commodity. Many times people try to participate in both aspects at once.

This distinction is not splitting hairs. The etymology of labor, *trabajo, travail,* etc., always points to hard effort, pain, and suffering. My self-actualization is something other than bartering off my abilities for estranged purposes.

At the same time, I am not able to answer the quite common and legitimate question concerning my "work, thought, and problem-solving models." I do not feel it necessary to employ models for my thoughts. I am criticizing the philosophical point of view that originated with Plato, which presumes that thinking occurs in paradigms and patterns. This kind of mental activity is at best a calculating, a concluding, a deducing from a series of axioms, which have been postulated or allegedly discovered. I am convinced that thinking by means of models is only like traveling by train or car. One needs tracks or roads for it, and those then condition—if not control—where one goes. Certainly one travels very quickly that way, but one is using an old path, used many times before, which prescribes where to go.

The idea of having to think by means of models involves belief in Plato's world of ideas, though they may be called simply laws of nature or viewpoints. Yet as the *Dhammapada* tells us: "In heaven there are no pathways." *"Caminante, no hay camino; se hace camino al andar,"* Antonio Machado writes: "Pilgrim, there is no path; you yourself are making it by walking." Thinking is not what people call research today. True thinking blazes trails. I do not experience life or reality as a riddle, which requires problem-solving strategies. My kosmology [sic] is different. I view reality neither as an *object* (latin *objectum,* "that which is thrust at me" [or "that which I throw"]) nor as a *problem* (greek *pro-ballô,* again "that which is thrust or held against me" [or "that which I throw"]). By kosmology I mean not a doctrine of the cosmos but the awareness of the experience of the cosmos's addressing me (*kosmos legein*).

Furthermore, it is difficult for me to discern authentically "how my work influences others." I say authentically, because I could very easily come up with a convincing reply. And this reply might not be completely untrue either, but it would result from my presumably eastern disposition, which instinctively gives only the kind of reply that satisfies the questioner, one that proceeds subjectively and not according to the laws of objectivity. In this respect, I might say that many of my ideas have entered the mainstream of the contemporary view of reality, that many ideas which I introduced decades ago have now emerged as generally accepted truths, not related to my person, and as self-evident ideas. I could mention the field of interreligious dialogue as one case in many.

For clarity's sake, I should be permitted to make a comparison, for which I myself take responsibility without wanting to draw anyone else into it. I know many theologians who have the intriguing zeal of reforming their churches or denominations, especially the roman catholic church. Their interest is one of genuine pastoral care. I am all for that. I am on their side, engaged in the same battle for justice, freedom, courage, and transparency—in short, a battle geared toward cleansing our old church in accord with the theological principles and claims of the same church. I admire these friends of mine and try to cooperate on this task with many of them. But if asked on a deeper level about my personal interest, I would reply that my foremost goal is not the reform of the church but the transformation of myself, of my self—though I am aware that one leads to the other and that neither one can be separated from the other. The point is certainly not a selfish concern for my *ego,* not an individualistic reaction to my subjectivist nature, not a conviction that spirituality is to be supranatural. I want to emphasize that. It is not a question of internal versus external activity, of *actio* versus *contemplatio;* neither is it a question of giving one set of procedures priority over another. I assume that most of us have overcome and are beyond such dichotomies. The difference lies in what I have called *kosmology,* the myth of the cosmos, of reality as it appears to and addresses us. The difference is, strictly speaking, not one of opinions but one of styles of thinking. Hence, our respective universes differ. I am fully aware that by making such statements, I am representing only a minority in the western world—west being meant here in a cultural, not a geographical, sense.

One can presume that basically such thinking cannot be explained sufficiently clearly because one cannot imagine a universe apart from one's own. Perhaps I should simply say that I do not believe in the myth of history as the sole area of reality, that death does not lie *ahead* of me. But by choosing the starting points of the west when expressing myself, I am already betraying the impossibility of my undertaking.

About the Person

Still, I do not want to dodge the first question concerning the "critical events" of my life. First, I am not aware of any sort of traumatic experience, either positive or negative. I cannot remember a conversion experience or an abrupt turning point in my life. Throughout life I have hardly dreamed; that is, I can hardly remember any dream. Furthermore, I cannot say anything unusual about my childhood.

It is possible that nothing seemed to impress me because I was extremely attentive, almost sensitive, to all events in my life. Everything seemed to impress me, perhaps equally strongly, yet deeply nevertheless. I have never been interested in exploring my life in a psychoanalytical fashion. Once an occurrence has been absorbed, it becomes part and parcel of my life and is thus indistinguishable from the rest.

Still, I can highlight a few events, which might be guideposts for the emerging of my ideas. I name them without seriously weighing the effects they have had on me. I must acknowledge that I am still quite self-conscious and uncomfortable about recounting personal experience, and it is likely that I will blur the "objective" picture. My reticence resembles that of a person who has endured torture and is now unable to describe her feelings and the details of that suffering.

Without having had to experience a war or having been in military or paramilitary service, my life still has been marked by wars. My birth coincides with the end of World War I. Then, in 1936, the Spanish Civil War interrupted my life, both externally and internally. Many of my classmates were stationed at this front or that; some of them died there. Three years of Nazi Germany up to two months before war broke out in September 1939 let me see the brutality of this military regime. Once safely back in Spain, I suffered from the knowledge that classmates were scattered across many different fronts and that familiar cities had been bombed. Another experience was the spanish dictatorial rule.

My stay of more than ten years near the shores of the Ganges certainly influenced my life also to a great extent. There I experienced the human condition in its barest form. I realized that humanity is not just of one kind, that the centrism of the west is only a singular and an almost minority perspective. I saw how fulfilled one person's life can be, presupposing that there is a faith, and with what little external comfort life can be lived to the fullest. For more than a quarter of a century, my stay in the indian world reassured me of what had only been an uncertain gut feeling since birth: Human self-identity is transcultural and thus cannot be determined by a singular point of reference.

My academic work in the United States taught me something else again. It showed me how different the "new world" is from the old world in Europe, how impossible it is to compare the east with the west—and vice versa. For another quarter of a century, I have been "commuting" between one of the richest cities of one of the richest states of the most powerful nation in the world and its opposite (twelve hours of time difference away), one of the most chaotic cities of one of the most "underdeveloped" states in one of the poorest countries of the world (disregarding the tiny minority of the rich). I have been commuting between Santa Barbara in California, U.S.A., and Varanasi in Uttar Pradesh, India. In a quite literal sense, my interior life was the only realm common to both hemispheres of life.

Without such experiences (or similar ones) it is hardly possible to overcome the trend in modern culture by which many are enticed into believing that human development has followed one single course and finds its climax in the achievements of the *homo technocraticus.*

In my own way, I have found myself not between but in the middle of the east and the west, namely, its hindu/buddhist and its christian/ secular versions, both of which have become part of my personal universe. As far as anecdotes from my life and so-called religious experiences are concerned, I would rather keep quiet.

In terms of my "audience" I could also give a standard answer and explain who my readers are, since I know that my condensed style of writing is intelligible only to a limited number of intellectuals and interested people. But my most serious answer will say that the "audience" I have in mind is the *dharmakāya,* the Body of Christ, the *karma* structure of the world, the Thou-character of reality, to use different idioms. More than thirty years ago, Svami Abhishiktānanda (Henri Le Saux) and I had conversations like this: If we *as christians*—that is, without any kind of apostasy or any superficial syncretism—could succeed in undergoing the *advaitic* experience, as it is lived in the best of hindu traditions, then *christians,* at least those of indian origin, would be automatically enabled to live an *advaitic-christian faith,* which makes possible both a fully hindu and a fully christian life—without the hard and painful experience of a split personality. Moreover, hinduism and christianity could then encounter each other thoroughly. No longer would it be necessary to write books about this encounter, to seek the recognition of bishops, or to organize colloquies. The genuine experience would suffice. We did not have in mind an "audience," a certain group of people. I recall a biblical passage which had also moved Augustine: "A number of sages is the salvation [*sôtêria*] *of the world*" (Wisd. of Sol. VI:24, 26; cf. Augustine, *De Trinitate* XIV, 1.) There exists, on the one hand, an internal river within reality, which makes epiphanies happen here and there whenever the soil has been prepared. But, on the other hand, I certainly have nothing against books, bishops, and colloquies.

The area of academics, the church, the state, and, moreover, the socio-economic, industrial complexities have their own subtle ways of having the rules of their game passed on, to set the boundaries within which discussions, dialogue, order, and courtesy rules can take their course. These areas are a part of what I would call the prevalent myth of our accepted cosmology.

I am neither a dissident nor a heretic, neither an anarchist nor a dropout. But I am defending the possibility of playing fair without having to accept the externally established rules. In other words, I am concerned with questioning the myth, the boundaries, the cosmology, without automatically having to become a "terrorist." Every society, every individual, and every culture has its own assigned boundaries of what can be tolerated. And I believe that my best service to our time, which is, in my personal view, entwined with a monocultural, technocratic civilization, could consist in defending pluralism. Pluralism is not synonymous with tolerance toward a multitude of opinions. Pluralism climaxes in acknowledging the unimaginable, that which is absurd for me and, to a certain degree, unbearable to me. These flexible boundaries are the boundaries of pluralism. Everything circles around being aware of our contingency. Pluralism dethrones monism and, with it, monotheism. Reality does not need to be transparent and intelligible in itself.

Who is my audience? It took me a long time to understand that the "public" I am writing for is the same that I am living for: humanity at large. This kind of public is not an abstraction. It is the *corpus mysticum,* the *dharmakāya,* the entire *karmic* net with its foundations, the entire reality. Did I not define the person as a knot in the net of relationships? The net stretches to the farthest corners of the world, as the *Rig Veda* says (I,164,34), and it depends on the density (wisdom) of the knot whether it can take part in the wholesome stretching of the net. It took me a long time to realize that most people have a firmly established environment, be it in form of their existential labors in daily life or in form of ideals for which they live: family, party, association, scientific or professional society or area of schooling, tribe, nation, or church. They live and write for a specific audience, and this is very effective. They are keeping in mind a special group of people and concrete problems; their language is well coined and to the point; they always have a partner in dialogue. These people live in their specific world; they have an environment they can handle. If I were cynical, I would point out the danger that they are simply feeding the market—the market of today's mass media.

Yet I do not have this kind of constituency, this clientele. At first glance, I should regard this fact as an obstacle. The lack of a certain public has led me to write in six or seven different languages. In spite of my grammatical imperfections and mistakes—technical errors, so to speak—I have always felt that each language is a world of its own. It may have some correlation with another world, but it can never match the other. Every word has its own home. That is the reason why my written work is so different from my spoken word. When speaking I identify—or, at least try to—with my particular audience, and I use language that seems appropriate for the situation, or better, which is the one offering itself to me. I can spontaneously conduct a catholic liturgy, give a hindu *upadesha,* engage in a simple conversation, deliver an academic lecture, present a philosophical meditation, and so on.

But when writing I sense a kind of common bond with all of humanity, especially with the culture of the present and the traditions of those streams of the past with which I am familiar. I try using the language and expressing the experiences that make me feel a part of the rest of humanity. Still, I am fully aware that my language is not universal and never will be. My language is tainted by time, place, culture, and my personal limitations. I rewrite my manuscripts six times or more. My affection for the *etymos,* the origin of words, is a result of the desire to express an original human experience, though these expressions certainly seem tainted by the colors of my particular situation.

That may be the reason why I instinctively allow my manuscripts to "lie around" for many years before I decide to publish them. Often this happened not intentionally, but was conditioned by circumstance and my urge to complement, to supplement, to see the other side, to expand my perspective, and similar things. It is something over which I have very little control. After the fact, of course, I could defend my position and attribute special value to it.

As bombarded as we are by journalistic texts (magazines, "daily" press), we still have, I believe, room enough to reflect on things not based on the latest news and their immediate effects. It may make sense that for ten years I have not been reading the newspaper, listening to the radio, or watching television. It enables me to listen to the voices of the voiceless and to the heartbeat of reality.

My audience is most certainly those people that *listen* to me. But I have the impression that even my contemporaries have something in them which transcends the fast-flowing river of passing feelings and sense perceptions. I am not writing for the future, let alone for eternity. I most certainly am writing for my contemporaries, though not exclusively for those of one continent or of one tradition—as long as the subject does not call for that. But I believe that we all are contemporaries (not chronologically but kairologically) of the entire world population, of the cosmos, and that we are, in a kind of cosmic synchrony, representing entire reality. I believe there is a quite contingent and imperfect, partial and limited expression for this something that does not exist without all its manifestations, yet does not exhaust itself in them either. Each of my words includes, points to, brings near, and symbolizes this mysterious abyss, this deity, this emptiness (*shūnyatā*), present to us in all that is—no matter how clumsy and crude my words may be. This may be the primary reason for my antipathy to writing about specifically "spiritual" subjects, thereby making these just another speciality. The "immortal" center, the "divine spark," the *ātman* is not a speciality which can be located in a certain spot.

There is an academic way of formulating this principle, but it does not satisfy me. One might argue in an erudite manner that my world is the universe of the great masters, that my "partners in dialogue" are, for example, Heraclitus, Plato, Aristotle, Thomas, Hegel, Heidegger, the authors of the *upanishads,* or Shankara, Abhinavagupta, Lao-tzu, Shinran, and others of such caliber. That would not be quite correct because I have to admit with embarrassment that I have not read enough of nor studied enough of these great minds. Unfortunately or not, I never had one single master. I touch upon the same subjects these masters have been dealing with—at least, that is what I believe. Yet I did not follow their footsteps; I did not belong to one of their schools, though I certainly can find many of their influences in my thoughts. Instead, I am moved by the same problems as they were, and I find myself in an intimate bond with most of them. I might say that I have been so captivated by the problems themselves that I have forgotten any concrete external guidance. In this sense, I might say that I am "autodidactic"—though I spent my entire life learning about every corner of the world and, thus, had many teachers.

This does not mean that my audience is the kingdom of ideas or the timeless universe of abstract ontological speculations. Be it the concepts of war and peace, economy, ecosophy, religion, nonviolence, technology, humanity, humankind, even divinity and nature, all these are for me not disembodied concepts of purely "theoretical" nature.

The Wisdom of Love

At this point, as I am revising a few pages written more than a decade ago, I would like to express the same in more academic words and clothe it in a proper philosophic garb.

1. To me, philosophy is just as much the wisdom of love as it is the love of wisdom. And true love is not only spontaneous but also ecstatic—that is, nonreflective. It does not revert to a critical analysis of itself. It does not know a why. As soon as I am able to give the reason for my love, loving no longer is authentic, no longer ultimate. One is a philosopher in the same way that one is a lover. In both cases one is affected by something. Philosophy is a primary, not a secondary, conviction: "Whoever is cursed by God to be a philosopher" is one! Philosophy cannot be manipulated, neither by the will nor by reason. Both the will and the intellect are means and tools, but they are not masters. Still, philosophy is a curious kind of love. It is wisdom, the wisdom of love, the wisdom contained in love. Philosophy is not simple *eros* or *agapê* or *bhakti* or *prema*. It is the kind of *sophia* (*jñāna*) contained in the original love. It is both transparency and enlightenment of self, *svayamprakāsha,* of the initial and all-conceiving *kāma,* of the impulse, *nixus,* of the urge, of the act, of the *karman* of reality. And wisdom evolves when both love for knowledge and knowledge about love coalesce.

Then authentic philosophy will crystallize into a life-style. To say it better, primal philosophy becomes the expression of life itself as articulated to reality or, rather, as written down with a *stylus* (a pen), the style of one's personal life. In my opinion, the kind of philosophy that solely deals with structures, theories, ideas; the one shying away from life, circumventing the practical aspect, and repressing feelings, is one-sided, because it does not touch upon other aspects of reality, and because of that, it is poor. Reality as such cannot be grasped, comprehended, and *realized* by a single sense organ or by only one of reality's dimensions. Such an approach would turn philosophy merely into another science—perhaps a more general science, a new form of algebra—but it would destroy philosophy as *wisdom* and prevent philosophy from expressing itself in human life-style. For that reason, all traditions require a pure heart, an ascetic spiritual attitude, an authentic life as the foundation for genuine philosophic activity. Philosophical activity requires all of it. A morally bad person may be a good mathematician, but cannot be a philosopher— at least not in an existential sense. A zen master might say: Only when being yourself—your pure self—will you understand things the way they are. This relatedness of philosophy to wisdom or experience simultaneously includes and transcends what the western world since Kant calls the critical aspect of philosophy. Every critical analysis has to end somewhere in the form of an ultimate experience, and it is here, at the seat of wisdom, that philosophy is born. I did call it *sophodicy* in former years.

The influence of the natural sciences on philosophy and on philosophical method has been so decisive that today not only academic philosophy itself but also ecclesiastical theology has become a special branch with special sub-branches. In the process, wisdom was either lost or degraded to an uncritical, naïve—if not primitive— contentedness with the world. Here one sees again the fatal split of reason and faith, of science and religion, of "philosophy" and "theology." One is satisfied with the argument that the law of morality applies to everybody, as if morality could speak on its own behalf, independent of any worldview and immune to any critical examination.

The traditional name given to a mentality that is clairvoyant, critical, intellectual, and equally spontaneous, free, and existential is wisdom—also, philosophy. If we do not restore harmony between this split, our civilization will go under. My philosophical desire is to offer a convincing alternative to the destructive schizophrenia of our prevalently technocratic culture.

I cannot elaborate here on this *manuductio artium scientiarumque ad sapientiam* (bringing both the arts and the sciences up more closely to wisdom). Instead, I should continue the more general train of thought.

2. How can I state my philosophy without thereby prejudicing it? The moment my life-style is no longer spontaneous, my pen no

longer free—because it may no longer be pure or it may be determined by external factors—my philosophy ceases to be authentic. Can I be a witness unto myself after all? Can I be critical of myself? Can the self remain the acting and knowing one when it becomes what is handled and known? Would I not clog the source, were I to return to it? "How can you, dear, understand the one who understands?" one *upanishad* asks (BU II,4,14). I could indeed retrace my life's journey; yet I am only able to see the footsteps when no longer standing in them. Therefore, I doubt the feasibility of making a personal statement about myself. *No word be spoken, unless it has become flesh!*[3]

Perhaps, though, I can do something else: recalling the burden carried along during my pilgrimage uphill and seeing whether I can make it lighter by throwing off unnecessary ballast.

3. As long as I can remember, I have felt a great need to encompass reality, or better, to become reality—to live. Thus, all my life I have been dealing with ultimate questions—not in a purely theoretical manner but by fully participating in them as a person. After studying extensively the speculations concerning the Ultimate throughout human history, I was so filled with the desire to seek what was real beyond its appearances that I felt tempted to abandon the part of reality related to my this-worldly activities. I was tempted to become either a specialized academic or an a-cosmic monk; I sensed the appealing and attractive power of both paths, purely intellectual abstraction and uncompromising asceticism. If I have now taken the academic as well as the religious path, then it is only because a professor is in my opinion not a business person but a "confessor" who makes a "confession," a confession with one's own life. Moreover, a monk should not be a loner, a *monachos,* but one struggling to be unified within, *monos:* alone, as all-one. Especially in this regard, I sense my calling to a synthesis, to having an all-embracing, wholesome mental attitude. The christian doctrine of the resurrection of the body has become a living symbol to me. Nothing of what exists must be lost; the real cannot be dissociated from the bodily. Indeed, it cannot exist without matter, though it does not consist of matter only.

4. My academic studies began with matter. For seven years, both physics and chemistry were my most serious intellectual occupations.

On the side, I started studying philosophy, but not because I had become disillusioned with my scientific studies. There certainly existed a continuity of interests. My philosophical *pathos* had been present all along; however, it took patience to enable me to follow these interests in an intense and systematic fashion. All that led to years of strictly philosophical studies and intellectual activity. The linear structure of the written word forces me to write about my theological studies only in the third place; but again, this interest has been present since my early conscious life. There was neither a break nor a sudden turning point, but even the word "theology" soon became too small to describe my interest and involvement, my total absorption in life, as a fully valid communion with reality. To me, this point is the religious urge; I understand religions as different paths by which people *believe* they are led to fulfillment, to happiness, or to liberation. Rather than understanding religion as something that ties us back (*religat*) to what concerns us greatly, the Ultimate Concern, I view it as something offering us freedom and joy, an unconditional, ultimate freedom from worries: I view religion as what liberates us, as an Ultimate Concern.[4]

The truly religious person is not the one saying "Lord, Lord," but the one overcoming the split between Man and World in an existential manner. Only in this way can we experience transcendence: "Lord, when did we see you naked, hungry, in prison?" (Matt. XXV:37–40). The ineffability of God can only be safeguarded by not talking about it. The idea of transcendence either destroys thinking or eliminates transcendence. At this point I could not do with only a purely theoretical gesture but had to embrace the life-style of a student of the kind of wisdom that moves humanity, the Gods, and the universe: "Here I stand, I cannot do otherwise!"

Now, leaving my confession aside for the moment, I want to say something about my profession: about that which I profess as my convictions, that is, about that which has subdued me—convinced and subdued (*convictus*) me in my struggle with reality—although reality has not always appeared, as in the Bible, in the form of an angel.

I would like to sum up my philosophical life according to three headings: *the existential venture, the intellectual burden, and spiritual freedom.*

The Existential Venture

5. The *existential venture* is the venture of a life at home in more than one culture and religion; it is the venture of an existence active in orthopraxy just as much as in orthodoxy. Personal circumstances (of biological, historical, and biographical nature) prompted me to *accept* the venture of a conversion without alienation, of appropriation without repudiation, of synthesis without syncretism, of symbiosis without eclecticism. In the process, indic teachings concerning one's personal *karma* (*svadharma*) became to me a new, vivid symbol. It certainly is not the case that I consider myself deliberately both indian and european, both hindu and christian, or that I artificially proclaim myself as both a religious and a secular person. Instead, my birth, my education, my initiatives, and my practical life have *made* me the person I am, nurtured by the basic experiences of both the western and the indic traditions. Thus, I am participating, on the one hand, in both the christian and the secular realms and, on the other, in both the hindu and the buddhist. (It took three fourths of my life to be able to express this view with confidence.) I realize the risk involved in doing so, but the challenge remains. The mutual understanding and enrichment among different traditions of the world can only take place when people, in an effort that helps them endure the existing tensions and avoid schizophrenia, are willing to sacrifice their lives and at the same time to maintain the polarities without falling victim to a personal or cultural paranoia. Only such a tolerant attitude of acceptance makes it possible—and that is the second step—for necessary changes to be able to occur. An *inter*cultural dialogue is not a purely political necessity or a purely academic affair. It is a personal affair and has to begin with an *intra*religious experience. If I am not personally suffering from the painful tensions and polarities of reality, if I only see one side from the inside, the other from the outside, I will not be able to understand fully. That means that I will not be able to face reality under the influence of both sides and will not do justice to both.

Another way of expressing this view would be by mentioning my interest in the *mythos* and my trust in the spirit. *Mythos* has guided me in two ways: first, it taught me to accept the *dharma* of my concrete existence (more than just choosing it); second, it taught me to dedicate myself to living a new kind of spirituality. This kind of spirituality attempts a dialogue among the basic elements of human nature: this dialogue is not solely or primarily rooted in the *logos* but, just as fundamentally, is rooted in the spirit. Western tradition leans toward a "crypto-subordinationism," which cannot be overcome even by the largest number of otherwise-well-argued pneumat*ologies,* let alone through phenomen*ologies.* Spirit cannot be reduced to *logos;* neither can it be subordinated to it. A phenomen*ology* of the spirit, of spiritual reality, is as incomplete as a ballet performance without music. The human organ for the spirit is the *mythos.* Both *mythos* and *logos* belong together. Yet their relationship is neither dialectic nor mythical; instead, each one comes into being through its connection with the other. If this connection were logical, it would suffocate the spirit in the *logos;* if it were mythical, it would reduce the *logos* to mere spirit.

In other words, there is no *logos* without a *mythos*—whose language is the *logos.* And there is no *mythos* without the *logos*—whose basis is the *mythos.* The no-man's-land of their relationship is completely empty. Neither rules the other. Here the buddhist *shūnyatā,* radical emptiness, became a lively symbol to me. Only pratītya-samutpāda, the radical relativity of all that exists, can maintain a harmony without prerogatives. I have said at various points that the scientist experiments with objects, or with parameters that correspond to these objects; the philosopher with ideas; and the monk with himself. I have the impression that I have lived through all these stages, and it seems that the third stage carries with it the heaviest burden in the existential venture. Here one risks one's life—at times, one's career and prestige, and even one's reputation.

In order to be authentic, the experiment must be also an experience; it must originate in the deepest corners of "one's personal" being. One must do it almost as if one could not take responsibility for it, without foreseeing the consequences.

I remember having spontaneously avoided situations where I could have acquired honors and power. I have never regretted avoiding these, but I must admit that I thought about them in weak moments. The idea of becoming a political figure, a bishop, a general director, or something like that is not always unpleasant. It took years before I could even mention this. And I still suppress here a page of my original manuscript.

The Intellectual Burden

6. The *intellectual burden* is not easier to carry than the existential venture. It consists of expressing these basic existential experiences in an intelligible way. Is it possible to pour the multitude of one's personal experiments and experiences into an intelligible mold? One could rephrase this question as whether it is possible to overcome the dilemma between monism and dualism in the existential as well as in the intellectual spheres. Here is the best place for the notion of *advaita*. By that I mean the immediate experience which opens up to us a reality where differences are not absolutized (dualism: God—world; matter—spirit), not ignored (monism: pure materialism, pure spiritualism), not idolized (pantheism: everything is divine and solely that), not reduced to mere shadows (monotheism: one single principle, one ruler, many subjects). A *polarity able to endure tension* is the ultimate characteristic of what is real. I would like to mention here the symbols *secularity, advaita, and trinity*: Time and timelessness are related and correlate; intuition about the ultimate is nondualistic; reality is trinitarian.

It is impossible to elaborate on this intellectual task in detail here. I will limit myself to a few pointers.

(a) The concept of *ontonomy* (*nomos tou ontos*) relating to both the internal and the constitutive *nomos* of every being, contributes to mutual understanding and enrichment among the various areas of human activity and spheres of being. It does so by providing (ontonomic) growth without a breach in harmony. This concept seems to me important for politics, economics, science, metaphysics, religion, and life itself. It highlights neither the loose and severed independence of individual fields (autonomy) nor the domination of the so-called higher classes over against the weaker and smaller ones (heteronomy). Instead this concept highlights a mutual relationship, a radical relativity (*pratītyasamutpāda*), which shows us that reality is ultimately a nondualistic polarity and that therefore it is best for every living being to seek a harmonious integration in the whole (ontonomy). In our ecologically disturbed world, we are beginning to accept that it cannot be in the United States' best interest to use more energy than any other country; that it cannot be advantageous to any single nation to become the strongest military power in the world; that it cannot be reasonable to practice a libertarian *laissez-faire* or to introduce artificial measures; that limiting freedom provokes rebellion; that encouragement of anarchy provokes totalitarianism; and so forth.

Is it possible to find an ontonomic order? In this respect, the symbol is the *person,* in my opinion. Is it not with the person that the person's mystery (which is neither singular nor plural) rests? A person is the conjunction, the uniting of all pronouns. If I hurt the I, the You will suffer. If I honor the son, the mother will rejoice. Developing such an ontonomic condition, where the optimum is not necessarily the maximum, is not only a science but also an art. At this point, theory needs *practice* and, on top of that, *poiêsis,* creativity: it is not technology that is needed here but *techno-culture.* The latter should not be confused with technocracy, where technology's power, not the art of *technê,* expresses itself.

(b) I would like to introduce here, along with the so-called ontological and theological differences, another ultimate and hence irreducible difference: the *symbolic difference.* The latter shows the symbolic structure of reality as a whole and hence is in a position of overcoming the dichotomy between subject and object on the cognitive level as well as the ontological level. A symbol is not another "thing," as, for example, a sign (which has a noetic nature). A symbol is simply an epiphany of what appears in the symbol itself. To confuse the symbol with the thing is as wrong as confusing the thing with the symbol; yet neither symbol nor thing is a separate entity. The symbol is neither on the side of the object nor on the side of the subject; instead, it has an equal relationship to both. Viewing existence as a symbol opens, in my opinion, a new chapter in the encounter of cultures and worldviews.

(c) A third neologism enables me now to sketch briefly a circumstance, quite important for understanding Man and the variety of cultures and religions. Phenomenology has made it possible for us to understand quite diverse contents of consciousness by means of an adequate *epochê* (placing in parentheses the question of the factual existence and interpretations of all the data of consciousness), thereby attaining intelligible *noêmata* (units of intellectual perception). Correspondingly, we need *pisteumata* in order to understand the ultimate phenomena of religious beliefs. Two assumptions are made here: first, faith is a fundamental, basic phenomenon of the human being; second, the human self-understanding is a fundamental element of Man's essence (different from the essence of an objectifiable "thing"). Therefore, one needs to know first what Man believes itself to be in order then to be able to understand what Man is and hence, to a certain degree, a person's beliefs as well. We should not underestimate the "methodical" difficulties involved here.

(d) Furthermore, my studies on the various relationships among cultures have led me to the notion of *diatopical hermeneutics*. The latter differs from the morphological as well as from the diachronic types of hermeneutics. The difference is that diatopical hermeneutics starts out with the awareness of the *topoi* (the loci of the various worldviews), which normally could not be understood within the categories (tools of understanding) of only one tradition or culture. While morphological hermeneutics unfolds the hidden treasures of a certain culture, and while diachronic hermeneutics bridges the temporal gap in human history, diatopical hermeneutics attempts to blend fundamentally different human horizons. The first step here could be a *dialogical dialogue,* which penetrates the *logos* all the way to the *mythos* and, as such, differs from a merely dialectic dialogue. How can we participate in the self-understanding of another person? The problems in which one becomes involved here are gigantic. Again, we need a love marriage of *logos* and *mythos,* or of *ātmavāda* and *nairātmyavāda*.

(e) Another way of expressing the same insight is to speak of the *tempiternal* ("time-eternal") nature of reality. Secular culture is correct in saying that being and time are "coextensive," so that there is no being which remains untouched by time. However, the time aspect of entire reality is only *one* aspect of the *tempiternal* nature of all things. Reality is not exhausted solely by the temporal aspect; furthermore, reality is not temporal now and eternal "later." Instead, reality is *tempiternal,* both temporal and eternal at once. I speak here of a tempiternal dimension of reality rather than of time and timelessness. Time and timelessness are mutually exclusive; this means that they do not fit in the same category. Yet, time and eternity both belong together as the arch and the lyre, to use Plato's illustration. Reality is neither totally temporal nor totally timeless; it is tempiternal.

(f) Furthermore, I have been wrestling with trying to formulate what I now would like to call the *cosmotheandric* or the *theanthropocosmic* intuition. Reality is nondual, and all existence has three constituting dimensions: the cosmic, the human, and the divine; one might also say, the material (space-time), the intellectual (conscious), and the mystical (eternal). After holding the mythical-holistic worldview for a time, people are now trying—and have been for the past three thousand years—to grasp reality by means of splitting, abstracting, and specifying it. Yet the time has come when the fractured pieces of these partial insights must be put together in a new, holistic worldview. There is no matter without spirit and no spirit without matter, no world without God and no God without the universe, and so forth. God, Man, and World are forms of the three original attributes of reality and not substances, artificially elevated as such. The three-world view (*triloka*), found in practically all traditions, should be synthesized into a view that does not overlook the insights of the previous analysis but makes possible the rediscovery of reality as a dynamic whole. There are not three separate histories or realms; instead, each realm penetrates the other two; each of these dimensions is present even in the smallest piece of reality. A concrete example from the area of religion that is intensely important today is viewing the various world religions as individual dimensions of the respective other. No single religion—not even all traditional religions taken together—has a monopoly on religion. Because of that, I have adopted the christian term *perichôrêsis* or *circumincessio,* which expresses the mutual penetration of the individual persons of the Trinity. Its buddhist synonym is *pratītyasamutpāda,* the radical relativity of reality. Apart from these, the shaiva concept of *sarvam sarvātmakam* (the universal relatedness of all to all), the wisdom of China, and many african traditions are pointing to a *theanthropocosmic* intuition.

(g) Later, I came to realize the central and ultimate nature of the *word,* possibly as the result of a long period of solitude. I realize the influence here of such people as Ebner, Heidegger, and Bhartrihari;

however, I have not studied these people's writings well enough to bring into the discussion my perception of their teachings. In this context, I would like to make the far-reaching distinction between terms as used in scientific language and *words* as symbols as used by authentic philosophy. It is from this point that I have worked out the *quaternitas perfecta* of the word, the fourfold aspect of the word: the speaker, the spoken to (the addressed), the spoken about (that *of which* is spoken), and the spoken with, language (*by means of which* is spoken); in other words, the I, the Thou, the It (meaning, idea), and the Whereby (matter).

(h) With that, another connection unfolds: The *word* reveals *reality's* cosmotheandric nature. By means of the polarity between being and speaking, the word overcomes the tension between being and thinking (the tension, forming the basis of western self-understanding—and the foundation of modern science). Being speaks. Our ultimate task is not to think being, thereby hoping to arrive at the truth; instead, it is to enable being to speak by means of an active listening and obedience on our part (obedience and listening are related in english [*ob-audire*] and in german: *Gehorsam* and *hören*). In place of the polarity between thinking and being emerges now the triadic relation of being, speaking, and thinking. We not only say what we think but also what we are. Being is not only thought of; it also speaks.

(i) Another important insight is what I call the *pars-pro-toto* effect. The latter can be applied to numerous contending ideologies. I have introduced this notion in connection with the encounter of religions. True ecumenism is not a reduction to one common denominator. Authentic tolerance does not require the dismembering of unacceptable viewpoints. Each tradition claims totality (*totum*) and searches for totality in its ultimate aspects. (Christ, for example, is not one *avatâra* among many; Shiva is not simply one God in the world's pantheon.) However, each tradition views the *totum in parte* and *per partem,* the whole in part and through a part, and it does so only in its respective proper categories, through its own window.

This concept, the whole as being viewed in and through a part, makes it possible, I presume, to reconcile the necessities for holistic thought and a holistic approach to reality with those of analytical thought.

(j) I could continue along these lines and explain the term *ecoso-phy,* as I have explained the other words I have introduced so far, or the term *theophysics.* But what has been said should be enough to illustrate the intellectual burden connected with the wisdom of love.

Spiritual Freedom

7. The section on *spiritual freedom* should have to be the longest of all because it cannot be summarized in words, because this part affects my life in particular. As long as one has not become liberated, one is not saved, one has not attained salvation, one has not experienced or reached *sōtēria, moksha, nirvāna.* In order to explain this state, one needs discipline and faithfulness; yet one is not obliged to a detailed exegesis. Thus, it might suffice to cite Paul's formula: Where the Spirit is, there is freedom (II Cor. III:17). The spirit penetrates everything because it is not someone's property. But I would rather let my personal life speak on that.

Once everything has been said and done, the source of it all remains, by necessity, invisible. What has been said results from a personal adventure, from an experience that is neither individualistic, undertaken for the sake of personal satisfaction, nor sociological, for the sake of proposing a new dream or a utopia for humanity. Instead, what has been said is what takes place in any small mirror that reflects all of reality and thus comprises the whole; it is what takes place in this intimate microcosm of the person, in this depth of the *contemplative love* to which I referred at the beginning of this book.

Questions and Answers on Life-style

You have mentioned along with the term "freedom" that in every person something unique, something eternal, is growing and that during this process the will does not play a decisive role. Can the person also miss this path by, for example, consciously refusing to accept grace?

Surely it is possible to miss this path. In this context, I would rather not emphasize the word "path," because true freedom is not one that has a predetermined path. We are free only because we make the path ourselves. Freedom does not consist in choosing between path A and path B but in landscaping a path where there has not yet been one. I must not be influenced in this endeavor from the outside, or else the path made is not a freely created, personal one.

To say it in a paradox: Freedom grows with the degree to which reality is acknowledged. Along the same paradoxical line, one might say about hell: Hell is hell primarily because its gates are wide open. Hell exists because one does not want to leave it—because one is filled with hatred: I want to scream, hate, defame; otherwise I would leave it.

There are three levels of freedom: First is the freedom of choice and the freedom of decision. Up to this point, we are within the psychological level. Second is ontological freedom, where the nucleus of my being creates its own destiny. We are simultaneously spectators and actors in this divine comedy of reality. Everyone plays a role. I can see both the others' playing and my own at the same time. I *am* the actor. I play an active role in the unfolding of the universe, in the history of people, in my family, in my village, in my country, in my own time, and so forth.

But then there is a third level, something we often forget: Not only are we watching and playing; we are also authoring. We are authoring the libretto of the "comedy." Though I am not the only author, I am still a co-author, so to speak. We are interpreting when watching the play and being part of it. We have the right to interpret and also the authority to do so; both lead to responsibility on our part. Hence, making mistakes does not mean that I was careless, that I did not play my part properly. Young people are very familiar with this principle. They know that life is not simply imitating, not simply repeating what they have already learned. Life is not to be ruled by the experience of the older ones, who now are a little wiser than they used to be, who know how to manage. Life is something brand-new; it is my inspiration, my creation, something that comes from within and which I myself do not know how to live out. On this third level, there is no libretto, no guideline, not even a learning from the past. For that reason, I myself am the first to marvel, to regret at times, to be full of tears at times because something fails. Yet at the same time I am full of joy because this small *me* is taking part in the I's role.

On this third, deepest level there are no models. The kind of spirituality that patterns its action according to what Jesus or Buddha or someone else might do is simply insufficient. It reeks of individualism and obsession with a disintegrated world. A Buddha, a Jesus, or an Einstein placed in my position no longer would be Buddha, Jesus, or Einstein. We are not chess figures. As impossible as it would have been for Buddha to be Buddha without his own time and environment, it would have been as impossible for me. Hence, the speculation of what Buddha might have done in my position is an inadmissible abstraction, a form of individualization, an extracting of myself from my own situation. This speculation rests on the false assumption that we are monads, actors with an assigned libretto. The anthropology of the *quaternitas,* portrayed in the previous chapter, tells us that we ourselves constitute place, space, and time, and hence we can never say what Jesus might do in my place. Otherwise Jesus would no longer be Jesus. It is *I* who am here now, and only I can do it. We are all at the same time, though not with equal shares, spectators, actors, and authors of reality.

Is it even possible to speak of missing the path? Could one say, perhaps, that the individual is not making full use of his or her capabilities?

This matter presents a paradox. One can make mistakes, but the mistake does not involve not following the libretto. Instead it involves not having been creative enough. There is a passage in the New Testament, not contained in all manuscripts but only in the best of them. There the Pharisees question Jesus about why he does not keep the sabbath. Jesus sees a farmer working on the sabbath and says to him: "If you are aware of what you are doing, you are blessed. If you are not aware of it, you are cursed and a law breaker" (Luke VI:5 D). If you are aware of the fact that today is sabbath and yet you are breaking the law, you are doing so at your own risk and have pondered it in your heart—then you are blessed! But if you say, "Oh, I'm sorry, I really forgot that today was the Sabbath!" then you are cursed. This is freedom.

Jesus says that the free transgressor is blessed. Christ himself was condemned by others for not keeping the sabbath. The kind of holy disobedience where one carries sole responsibility moves history. "Here I stand, I cannot do otherwise," Luther said. When I cannot do otherwise, then I am free. Otherwise it is only a matter of politics, adjustment strategies, and so-called compromises. I can always come up with arguments that will justify my actions, but the other kind of argument involves the creative acts of the person, the most dangerous ones we can do. These acts can prompt a schism, evoke a revolution. Yet these acts make for true human life; otherwise we are only dabbling in peripherals.

Does discipleship mean, then, that I must do my part and not do what Jesus has done?

Jesus or Christ is not a role model I have to imitate. By that I do not want to refute Jesus' immense magnetism or argue against our chance of learning from the great masters in general—and minimize our obligation. But the true *imitatio Christi* is not a replicating, an "imitation," but one's personal transformation in the person of Christ. Jesus is not a role model; yet Christ can become my own life. That is what mysticism teaches us.

The Eucharist means mainly that the body of Christ is *eaten* by us. It does not mean that *I* will turn into his body but that *his body* is transformed *within me,* thus becoming a part of me, as bread becomes a part of me when eating it. The Eucharist is not a trick: it is not Christ turning into bread but the bread being Christ. Thus it follows: "Whatever you have done for the least of these, you have done for me" (Matt. XXV:40). This is not an imitation, not a replica, but an embodiment, a transformation: not the *alter Christus* (other Christ) but the *ipse Christus* (Christ himself). Therefore, Paul views Christ as the head and us as the body. Christ's declaration that he is the bread of life (John VI:35ff.), the departure sayings (John XVff.), the Pauline passages, and all of christian mysticism help us see that the point is not to imitate Jesus but to embody Christ in ourselves. The relationship between Christ and christians parallels the relationship between Jesus and the Father; it resembles having a child, whereby begetting and being begotten are inseparably and dynamically interrelated. In this process, the Trinity is already contained.

We pray in the Lord's Prayer: "Your will be done." And Jesus said once: "It is my bread to do the will of the One who sent me" (John IV:34). How would you interpret that in light of what has been said?

I understand it in two different ways. First, the plea "Your will be done" is a very dynamic prayer. One can pray it in a meaningful manner only when it involves one's aim to resolve the tension and polarity of two wills becoming one. Otherwise it makes little sense to tell Almighty God: "Do as you please." God would reply, "I know that!" If God is almighty, God's goals will be reached; God does not need my devotion for that to happen. The plea makes sense only because *I* want it to be so. My will is to become part of this almighty will and I with it. I want to adapt not to the will of someone more powerful but to this creative will which, in christian parlance, reigns over this world. So I pray that I be allowed to participate in this free, forever newly creating will. Moreover, I dare to wish that this tiny will of mine may impress upon the other will. Hence, it continues: "As in heaven, so also on earth." It expresses the participatory, the synergetic nature of which Paul is speaking (I Cor. III:9; perhaps the same is meant in III John 9), the collaboration of God's will and mine: God's will is waiting for my will so that "as in heaven, so also on earth" may come true. The plea in the Lord's Prayer, then, is concerned not with fatalism nor with this meaningless redundancy sketched above.

Second, there are moments in human life—like Jesus' situation in the garden of Gethsemane—where my will wavers, my freedom atrophies and shrivels. I cannot take on too much at once. My will revolts against that. In such situations, it is beneficial and reassuring to know, on the one hand, that my will is not the only and governing one and, on the other hand, that there is a higher will to which I can turn and to which, in turn, I can submit my will. This is the human condition. It is not always possible to keep one's head in the clouds. Not everything in life is pure joy; not everything falls automatically into place. Life is challenge and tension. At the same time, it is realistic and comforting to know that we are not alone in this battle.

If evil and failure are part of the human condition, are there also such shortcomings in the divine realm?

Why do we want to lay all the blame merely on Eve and the serpent? The question is, Where does evil come from? Christian theology is quite often a little brittle here, unlike islamic theology with its doctrine of Satan, Iblîs. Islam has taken seriously the absoluteness of God as hardly any other religion has. So evil cannot be simply covered up as if it had emerged somewhere on its own. I can only summarize briefly here (my summary is based on a narrative by Husayn Ibn Mansûr Hallâj, translated by L. Massignon).[5] The narrative has a mystical viewpoint, similar to that of Maulânâ Jalâluddîn Rûmî, one of the other great poets of the islamic tradition.

Where does evil come from? From Satan. Who is Satan? The first creature God created. Satan has first place and is much higher, for example, than Mary. It is the first angel, the so-called Lucifer, and, apart from God, it is the most complete image of the divine. Everything else takes second place. Evil, as far as it is real, can only come from God. On the last level of reality where only God is, there is no evil. But within the destiny of time, evil is very powerful and real. As such, evil has the Almighty as its origin, although the highest being is the only one that does not commit evil.

God says within the circle of angels: The human being is to be higher than Lucifer, and the angels are to give honor to Man. Lucifer was the first one to have understood the implications of this command—it, the first-created in creation. Hence, a monumental dialogue ensues between God and Lucifer. The latter says:

> How can you expect me to give praise to a creature? How can I do this to you? How can I give honor to anyone else but you? I realize that my refusal will bring about my fate of being expelled from here, when being thrown into hell by you. I realize that through my refusal the entire universe will be restructured, changed. But I will remain true to you, in spite of yourself, in spite of your decrees, out of loyalty and love to you; after all, I am your most perfect image. I will not obey you! Only you can I worship!

Satan is like a rejected lover. When meeting Moses and telling him about its fate, Satan is reproached by Moses: "How can you disregard a divine command?" Satan replies: "It was only a test (temptation), not a command!" It does not view itself as a sinner: "First, I served God for my own pleasure, now I serve God for God's pleasure. I did not deny my destiny." And then comes a magnificent love declaration: Satan is always connected with God, and whenever

God's name is mentioned, Lucifer's name will not be forgotten either. Satan is proud of this. This is its consolation.

From Lucifer's tragic loyalty to its first promise to honor God and God only arises evil in the world. Therefore, tragedy is part of human history, not simply because the human being has sinned, as in christian theology, or because the angel has sinned also. The Fall (in which islam does not believe) is something that takes place within the whole. Thus, we have to realize our dignity and responsibility; all of that belongs together. It is what makes for our magnificence and responsibility, in which human life consists. We could learn from islam: the human being may have fallen; but the Fall occurred within time, and therefore the Fall will come to an end. That is salvation, reconciliation, the *anakephalaiôsis* ("recapitulation") in Paul's writings (Eph. I:10), the resurrection in Peter's (see I Peter I:3), the *apokatastasis*, the reconstruction, the reconstitution, the completion of the mystery of bare existence (Acts III:21). Salvation is just as much a part of us as sin.

You outline an incredibly proud, self-confident path for the human being. In this context, would it be reasonable to speak of a certain self-restriction on God's part? God actively shrinks, so to speak, in Jesus (in the sense of a "kenosis," a relinquishment of God), so that the human being can develop self-confidence.

It would be reasonable, but my intent is to overcome dualism without reverting to monism. Therefore, I would not view God and Man as being in competition. In order to acknowledge the unlimited dignity of Man it is not necessary to belittle God. It is not simply a matter of Man's chances and fate but also of God's. I am not monotheistic in the sense that I believe God is somewhere and then retreats a little and makes room for us.

I believe that in this particular view lies a radical break of christianity with the monotheistic tradition of judaism. The break consists in the doctrine of the Trinity, which says that God truly enters both the World and Man. The creative power of this break became visible only when christianity left the Mediterranean area and its colonies. As a result, the doctrine of the Trinity has led a shadowy existence for the first two thousand years and has never found active expression in the life of christians. As long as christianity does not muster the courage to part with the abrahamic sources, it will remain only a jewish sect; but then it had better leave Africa and Asia altogether because the colonial times are over. Such will be the great challenge for christianity in the third millennium, especially in Asia.

For that reason, I do not think much of the theologically clever thought concerning a relinquishment of God. I believe instead that God too participates and is included in this play. The point is not only our own destiny. I am convinced that if we indeed were, and were able, to totally destroy the earth, God too would be destroyed. I cannot believe that there seriously could be a doctrine that God takes on the human form if, at the end of time, the incarnation were to become merely a small episode concerning a man by the name of Jesus, who roved Palestine. Rather, I believe with Paul and the entire New Testament that Christ is the Alpha, the Omega, and everything in between, Beta, Gamma, Delta, and so forth, and that this mystery has made its appearance since the beginning of the world. I do not allow myself to be reduced in an infinitesimal fashion (a speck of dust in the universe)!—although we cannot discuss all that quickly.

Everything is interrelated, God, Being, the Trinity, Mary, and so forth. And this interrelatedness begins in our life, hence, with our attitude toward reality. When dealing in our own way with these basic questions, we will receive the gift of freedom. No longer will I be frightened by dogma. In an orthodox sense, a good christian is not even supposed to place faith in dogma. The latter is to be only the channel that guides the act of faith. When this channel is clogged by tradition, enlightenment, or whatever, faith will seek other channels. Thomas Aquinas says, "The act of the believer does not end with the doctrine but at the thing."[6] And the thing transcends all formulations. This is not a faith in doctrines. Doctrines are dependent on time; they express a certain understanding of a thing. They are a scaffold, nothing more; and we do not believe in scaffolds. At times, though, a scaffold as a tool is helpful; so perhaps we are now in need of some new scaffolds.

You said that in case of a destruction of the world also the divine or God would no longer exist. That means, conversely, that the divine is something immanent. We are always talking about the divine in terms

*of images and similes. But when questioning the subject-object differ-
ence as a certain model of perception, then the divine becomes sud-
denly something inside of us; it no longer remains something
transcendent. What are we talking about then?*

We have to be careful and avoid a misunderstanding. The divine
not only is immanent but also transcendent. It would be a great
mistake to reduce God, in an immanent theology, to something
purely secular. God is transcendent, but God's transcendence can
only be visualized when we, at the same time, visualize and emphasize God's immanence. The divine is also always immanent. That is
already implied in the logic of the term "transcendence." "Pure
transcendence" would be a contradiction in terms since the moment
I say that, I would already be proved wrong. After all, I arrived at
this conclusion by means of thinking. Therefore I said that the
thought of "pure transcendence" is full of contradictions and thus
unimaginable. In addition, our mental condition never will allow us
to pull all the strings, and our thinking is not absolute.

What I am primarily opposing is this superficial saying: "In the
end, everything will turn out fine because our dear Lord is around
and he will take care of it . . . ." That does not seem very convincing
to me. Likewise, it is wrong to spiritualize the divine completely so
that it is only left to be a part of the Spirit's immanence. I am
suggesting that the divine is present in the world in the same way that
I see us also being present in the divine. Here the belief in the
christian mystery is relevant. Christ is the symbol of the highest
reality. In Jesus Christ, the divine is *just as* transcendent as it is
immanent; the bodily in him is just as divine as it is different from the
divine. In Christ everything is divine—his walking, his eating, everything he does—and everything is at the same time human and also
material. This is the image of the divine as it presents itself, at least to
christians, in the mystery's entirety.

In summary then, there is no immanence without transcendence,
and there is no transcendence without immanence. Furthermore,
the divine must not be reduced to being a mere subject. The old split
of object and subject would then remain, only with negative
connotations.

In conclusion: My intent with these dialogues is not to develop a
new theological view. That would be meaningless in such little space.

Instead, I would like to make an experience communicable, to aid in this process—wherever help is accepted—so that the nucleus of our existence can be discovered. In this endeavor, I have purposely avoided using specifically christian language, which I could have done had I chosen to. I have tried to point to this prime experience of being human, which doubtless involves also the divine.

I should not skip your question, though. If Being disappears, if Man annihilates, I said, God also would cease to be Creator, would cease to be God. In our human language we may add that this "if" is uncomprehensible, and even that we cannot actually perform this thought. We know that Man is mortal and that the solar system will not subsist much more than 4 or 5 billion years. This was not my point. My tale was to affirm that we do not have, nor can we have, nor need we have any "assurance" that this "if" may not be an "if." Meister Eckhart also said something similar.

IV. Trisangam: Jordan, Tiber, and Ganges

*Does one need to be spiritually semitic and
intellectually western in order to be a christian?*

In this chapter on *three kairological moments in the christian
self-understanding,* I would like to summarize what I have been
doing and saying for almost half a century on being a christian
today.[1] My experiences and encounters on this subject are too
numerous to recount here,[2] and I should like to omit strictly theological problems also in order to concentrate on a general philosophical
description of the present state of christianity and at the same time
characterize in greater detail the "places" of wisdom.[3]

In the context of this book, this chapter has the task of describing
a deeply christian perspective which is linked to both wisdom and a
living philosophy. The question is how one can remain loyal to one's
tradition and prevent this tradition—and oneself—from becoming
absolutist as well as diluted. This question is necessary; otherwise there is the danger that all traditions, not only the christian,
become diluted into one general monoculture, which is the opposite of wisdom: Wisdom has lived-in rooms and not just a nice
façade.

The Dilemma

At the present time, humanity is facing a mutation, and contemporary theological reflection can no longer legitimately continue to
think within its usual categories. Problems have changed; central
questions have to be restructured—let alone the answers. That is the
reason why I am calling for a new council—not for a Vatican III but
for a second Council of Jerusalem (cf. Acts XV). For it, we would
need a certain idea of the world's situation as it is today and a

corresponding deeply christian perspective. I would like to concentrate here on the latter.

One might portray the history of the christian tradition in its relation to other religions by means of the three holy rivers named in the title of this chapter. Jesus was baptized in the Jordan, the *Hâ Yardên,* the *Nahr al-Urdunn* (see Matt. XXXI:13; Mark I:9). One cannot wash off the Jordan's water from the body of Christ—which also means from the body of christians.[4] Christian tradition is indelibly of jewish origin. Jesus, the disciples, and the Gospel writers were all jews. One cannot understand the Gospels without a quite distinctive jewish spirituality. By spirituality I mean here a series of *basic convictions* before they became manifest in theories and realized in practice. We are facing the question today: Can there be a single, universal spirituality—a fundamental human mind-set which is both universal and concrete? Can a spirituality of jewish origin offer such a possibility? Is the Jordan *the* river, as the Nile was for Egyptians?

Such theoretical questions have to be considered in light of twenty centuries of christian history, these being equally marked by the water of another holy river, the Tiber, *il Tevere, Tiberis.* Peter and Paul died at its banks, and it is here they continue to live on in history. Without Rome, christianity is also incomprehensible, even in its anti-roman aspects. The Mediterranean is the christian sea, the *mare nostrum,* "our sea." Christianity today is a more or less harmonious mixture of jewish heritage and greek, roman, gothic, and western elements. I would like to emphasize that we should neither overlook nor absolutize this fact. Christianity is the religion of these two rivers. We cannot do without them. But does it have to be that way always?

Just as christianity cannot secede *spiritually* from the Jordan, it would disintegrate *intellectually* without its connection with the Tiber; the latter I am using as a symbol for the western mentality in general, no matter how broad and multilayered it may be.

The question arises today whether the borders of christian theology have been definitely established by these two rivers or whether we should not cross another Rubicon first, this time not to defeat Pompey but to reach peacefully the Ganges.

The question is twofold: Either christians will have to acknowledge that they cannot conquer the world—and should not since they represent only one phylum among the peoples in the history of religions. How then could christians claim universality and insist on being the only true religion? Or there is, indeed, something in christianity that is specifically universal. If that were the case, could one see Christ as a universal symbol? In examining this twofold question, I refer to the *Gangā* since it appears useful as a symbol. The Ganges has many sources, among them one that is invisible. The Ganges disappears in a delta of countless river beds, and the Ganges has witnessed the birth of many religions along its banks. What draws me to the *Mā Gangā* (apart from a personal affiliation) is its multifaceted origin, the curious delta, and in particular this secret, heavenly source. In *Illahâbâd* (Allahâbâd), the old city with its islamic name, not only the waters of the *Jamunā* and of the *Gangā* lead into the *Prayāga* but also the invisible and divine *Sarasvatī*, both river and the Goddess of wisdom. For millennia, millions of people have been testifying to that in the famous *Khumba-Mela* by means of pilgrimages that are calculated every twelve years in astrological (and astronomical) fashion.

In no way should the *Gangā* help support an āryan ("indo-germanic") prejudice. Every country has its rivers, and most of them are sacred. The *Mā Gangā,* the mother river of the Ganges, serves not only as a symbol for hinduism, buddhism, jainism, sikhism, and the original religions of India but also as a symbol for all other traditions of Eurasia, Africa, America, and Oceania with their quite different forms of expression in both spirituality and mentality.[5]

The person rooted in such mentalities finds little meaning in common christian theology. Not only the contents of the Bible but also most of the christian presuppositions and ways of thought are foreign and confusing to those non-abrahamic traditions. I want to emphasize this fact explicitly. Although hardly 10 percent of the world's people are fluent in english (and even fewer in german or in any other european language), and although christians are a minority on this planet, the inhabitants of the "first world" are inclined to assume that what they are intending and thinking corresponds to universal patterns. There is a series of cultures caught in such a universalization syndrome.

We are left with two possible answers, both legitimate. Whichever we choose is more than just an individual religious decision. Whichever the christian body at large will prefer is a political decision of immense historical importance. Reality is not given all at once and for everyone equally. The future of religions also depends, among other things, on how the various religions view themselves and what kind of decisions they make. Christianity is *also* what christians make of it—and will make of it. Politics and religion have to be distinguished, but they cannot be completely separated.[6]

The first answer says that christians should give up their claim of universality, that christians should allow the rivers of the world to flow peacefully without pumping into them the christian waters and without redirecting christian rivers into the Dead Sea or into the Mediterranean, that they should not cross the Rubicon again and flood all countries of the world. Then christianity can be regarded as a religion among many, and Jesus, ultimately, as the savior only of christians. Then, christianity's relationship to other religions will have to be viewed as an interreligious problem, much like international affairs among sovereign states. In this case, christianity preserves its identity by distinction. It deduces its uniqueness by differing from other traditions, and this difference should be preserved.[7] The point of discussion here is not tolerance, mutual respect, and good neighborly relations; the point is solely that a certain kind of christian theology claims universality.

According to this first answer, christians should acknowledge other religions each in its own right. Since uncontrolled growth is cancer, a constantly growing, worldwide, unique christian religion would become a cancerous growth. Rivers should preserve their separate identities, and so should religions. The waters of the *Gangā*, of the *Huanghe*, or of the *Nahr an Nil* (Nile), according to the first answer, contain too much salt (or toxic substance, if you wish) and are too far away (philosophically, theologically, humanly) to be able to mix with the christian rivers; otherwise one would incur, to a great extent, both chemical and physical mutations. It is better, then, to keep them apart.

The second answer is probably the more common one, though often secularized in its weaker expression. This answer says that the claim of christianity's universality is fundamental, so that christianity without universality would be a negation of itself. It views christianity as a privileged phylum, called on to bring the world together, to "convert" the other cultural and religious rivers "into" a christian

Amazon, and to irrigate the whole planet—whereby christianity would become, of course, an even more universal religion than before. The second answer would argue, Who are we to stifle the growth of christian dynamics? Is not the temptation of every kind of revolutionary movement, as soon as its leader has assumed power, to quell any other development? Is christianity subject to such a temptation? Up to now christians have absorbed what is "good" in Mediterranean religions in a syncretistic way. Why could they not proceed this way with other religions?

The dilemma is the following: Many christians may feel that they are betraying their deepest faith convictions when surrendering the belief that the christian dimension is universal. But there are also a growing number of christians who are deeply yet painfully aware that the claim of universality is an imperialistic leftover whose time is up and that most followers of other religions perceive this claim as a threat to—and a disregard for—their faith convictions.

This chapter takes a courageous step toward a solution of this dilemma by showing that the rivers of the earth neither truly meet each other—even in the oceans—nor are dependent on such a merging in order to become life-giving rivers. The rivers do not meet, not even in the ocean. "They" meet each other nevertheless, namely, in heaven. "They" meet in the form of clouds after their initial transformation into vapor, coming down eventually as rain into the valleys of the mortals and nurturing the rivers of the earth. Religions do not grow into one, most certainly not in order to form one organized institution. They meet only after they have been transformed into vapor, after their metamorphosis into spirit, which then is poured down in countless tongues (cf. Acts II:3). The rivers of the earth are fed by the clouds' leaning down as well as by terrene and subterranean sources after they have undergone this other transformation from snow and ice into water. The true reservoir of religions does not only consist of the doctrinal water of theology; it also is composed of the transcendent vapor of divine clouds (revelation) and the immanent snow and ice of glaciers and the snow-covered mountains of the saints (inspiration).

My contention is that neither is the christic principle a particular event nor is it universal in the sense of a universal religion. What then is it? It is the center of reality—from the perspective of the christian tradition. This vision does not have an absolutely universal character. It is the christic universal vision. I will elaborate on this metaphor and try to show that no single religious tradition can have the monopoly on the living waters of the rivers (that is, salvation) and that we cannot dilute the doctrinal statements of any authentic religion for the sake of gaining religious conformity.[8] I have portrayed elsewhere the *pars-pro-toto* effect inherent in this problem.[9] My metaphor is not to express in an unspecified manner the transcendent unity of all religions. It may go in this direction, but I do not want to confuse the true rivers with chemically pure water. As waters differ, so do religions—each river carries with it its ordinate number of salts and micro-organisms. Moreover, we should not forget that water is undergoing a transformation (of death and resurrection—in form of vapor, snow, and again water), which is the reason why it can continue enriching the Earth.

Religions are not static constructs; hence, no religion should be afraid to let its water evaporate as the climate becomes unbearably hot. The clouds will bring it back as soon as the heat of polemics dissolves and the waves smoothen again. In other words, every water not only is unique but also contributes by its specific form, its taste, and its beauty to the religious spectrum. And this spectrum is not some kind of special sphere, but the entire world with its ultimate destiny. The meanders, the *ghats,* the ports, the bathing spots, the quiet ponds, the rapid cascades, the rough and stormy waters—all of these are part of the phenomenon of the religious. Whatever the "essence" of religion may be, living and real religions are not essences but concrete, powerful, and dangerous existences. Religious rivers are much more than the H_2O of chemistry.

Therefore, my method cannot be solely deductive. It also has to proceed in an empirical and historical fashion. Thus, before coming to any conclusions, I would like to, on the one hand, sketch the historical stages of christian self-understanding and, on the other, attempt a theological interpretation of these stages.

Five Epochs of Christian History

We should take seriously today's awareness that theological understanding always depends on temporal, contextual, and other parameters. It explains why christians have not always interpreted the basic christic principle in the same way.[10] The self-understanding of christians across their history can be summarized in five epochs, though the former epochs may continue to exist in the latter. For that reason, I do not call them chronological but *kairological* moments of christian history.[11]

1. The primary christian self-understanding of the first centuries was that of *witness*. Early christians did not consider themselves followers of a new religion. Instead, they testified to the living words uttered at the banks of the Jordan and confirmed by the resurrection. Early christian witnesses testified to something that had transformed their lives and remained a kind of suprahistorical event to them though it was fairly soon interpreted in different ways. They lived not merely in history; eschatology was an ever-present factor. Early christians could face death without fear. They were martyrs, witnesses of an event. Here the most important virtue was fidelity. This conviction was dominant up to the fall of Rome under Alarich's siege in 410 or up to the death of Augustine in 430. The true christian of that time was a martyr, that is, a testimony.

2. The next moment can be described by the word *conversion*. The world became "christian," but the atmosphere was still "pagan." Little by little, christians established themselves as a social and political reality. Yet they were still aware that Constantine's declaring christianity as the official religion had its pitfalls. True christians had to be different from "the world." Under such conditions, the true christian not only belonged to what had become the official religion, but also displayed a change of heart. *Conversio morum* (change of life-style) hence is the motto of the monks. The authentic christian may have dealings with the developing political order or may be attracted by the social force of christianity, but the true criterion is the life-style, the purity of the heart. Being a christian means being converted to Christ. True christians follow the monastic call—even in the world. In the meantime, however, christianity had produced not only a certain number of doctrines but also regulations of political nature. With this new self-understanding, christians determined that they were to form a religion, even a state, the nascent empire. This religion was not yet hostile toward other religions, especially when the latter were far away; yet conversion slowly

assumed a political connotation. Whole peoples were converted and continued to carry with them the basic convictions of their respective life-styles. Such was the destiny of a large number of european peoples. This development lasted up to the Middle Ages, though it was shaken by its conflict with islam, which produced a new attitude.

3. The word *crusade* characterizes the christian self-understanding of this new epoch. It began in the eighth century and lasted until sometime after the fall of Constantinople in 1453, possibly even until the defeat of the Turks at Lepanto in 1571. Christendom was by then firmly established. Even though there were battles and internal tensions among the christian princes, nothing determined christian life more than the notion of an external threat by islam, which became a collective obsession. After the battle of Guadelete in 713, Spain fell quickly under muslim domination, and southern France became "occupied" in similar fashion. Carl Martell is celebrated as the rescuer of (christian) Europe, but Jerusalem and the sacred places "fell" under muslim rule. Vienna was occupied. The christian empire had to assert itself; the danger was sensed everywhere. Often jews were made the scapegoats of christian frustrations. In this situation, the christian had to become a soldier, a crusader, a "militant" person, and these terms of old are used to this day. The superiors of these new religious movements no longer were called father, abbot, or mother, but general—and the movement itself becomes an "order." *Militia christi* (army of Christ) denotes the primary attitude of this epoch, either in the literal sense of the word crusader or—interpreted more eclectically—in the resolve to become a jesuit or some other warrior for Christ. ˙

The Reformation had similar traits: christianity was a challenging undertaking; it required courage, faith, decision. One had to become a christian knight, a hero; one's sacred duty was to conquer the outside world for Christ or to win it back to Christ. One must not compromise on worldly matters. Faith alone was sufficient. Therefore, islam, which was perceived as a threat (in part also as a portentous warning not to become lukewarm), became the image for all other non-christian religions.

In this epoch, christianity slowly developed the idea of being the only true religion, and all other religions were viewed as false. *Vera religio* (true religion) emerged as a sacred phrase whose meaning, "the true religious life," switched slowly to "the only true and salvation-bestowing institutionalized religion." This basic perspective persisted for several centuries. At a very distinct moment, however, something new happened in christendom—that is, in the *Sacrum Romanum Imperium Germanicum* (in the Holy Roman Empire of the German Nation). In 1492, a new continent was "discovered." Thus, the scenery changed: christendom as a world order collapsed and christianity as a religion evolved.

4. In this epoch, *mission* became the main characteristic of the christian religion all the way to the modern era. The zeal to conquer was irresistible. Yet the desire to conquer America could not be religiously justified by the term crusade. Amerindians could not be regarded as a threat, such as the muslims, nor did the former accuse christians of anything. The *conquista* could be justified only by saying that America had to be christianized. Salamanca, for example, boiled over with theological discussions. Bartolomé de las Casas defended the *indios*. Francisco de Vitoria tried his best. Yet the ideology prevailed that christians were obliged—or, better, had the *mission*—to proclaim the Gospel to, convert, and save the amerindians. This ideology continued to spread. Now the true christian was a *missionary*. Again, the connotation of this word changed from its literal sense of going out and preaching to the "nonbelievers" to the point where the christian became a mystical sacrifice, thus a role model to the world for the sake of salvation. Even Thérèse de Lisieux, secluded in a Carmelite convent, viewed herself as a missionary—and lived as one. The theology of mission became the most elaborate of theologies.[12]

Nevertheless, christians realized in their contact with other peoples of the world that these newly discovered religions contained a treasure of spiritual goods. As a result, a reevaluation process began. Names such as Matteo Ricci and Roberto de Nobili remind us of this process. Yet many efforts geared in this direction were suppressed. Christian institutions viewed them as stifling the dynamics of time, that is, the political expansion of the european states. Since these institutions called themselves christian, they could not tolerate theological interpretations that might undermine their own political splendor. The battle over the rites in China is a famous example of that. In short, christianity had a mission duty toward the whole world. To this day, christians are praying and paying for mission societies. Even political consulates are still called missions, and the term is commonly accepted. Yet two world wars, a hundred million deaths in these wars in our century, and the independence of well over 170 new states mark the end of this epoch. Many christians realize they no longer can "missionize" other peoples. We reach the present age.

5. After the dismantling of the colonial political order, the new catchword is *dialogue*. Now there is a trend toward christianity's meddling in and interacting with other cultures, toward its greater respect for other religions; there are even attempts of newly defining the term christian. Many christians no longer wish to conquer, nor even to convert; they wish to serve and to learn. They offer themselves as serious partners in open dialogue—though not without understandable distrust on the part of their opposites (one can understand this fact easily by being familiar with history). Today christians are saying that dialogue is not another strategy but an open process for mutual enrichment and for getting better acquainted with each other. Christendom has little prospect for the future; christianity is in a crisis; only the Christ symbol is still alive and well. So *christianness* emerges, namely, on the sociological level.

One thing is clear: The christic principle continues somehow to preserve the characteristics of these five epochs. One finds in all christians something of a *witness*. Christians are not comfortable without the view that they are somewhat better than non-christians (*conversion*); without the courage to confess their faith (as soldier, as *crusader*); without the feeling of being burdened with and responsible for the care of the entire world (*mission*). Aware of not being alone now, however, christians open themselves to *dialogue*. At this point in time, we are witnessing a new spiral turn in the interaction between christians and peoples of other faiths.

Lessons Learned from History

We should place our reflections in the respective historical context. The first epoch is still nurtured by the waters of the Jordan. The old covenant is considered here highly important. Thus, christians are still semites spiritually. The three ensuing epochs are nurtured by the waters of the Tiber. Thus, christians are intellectually europeans; they are primarily still related to the cultures of the Mediterranean. Across the Atlantic Ocean we find, in the historical sense of the word, only colonies, despite the fact that the two Americas, having lived independently for five hundred years, are now displaying more or less individual traits.

Only the fifth epoch with its viewpoint is no longer satisfied with merely exporting the Mediterranean culture. It longs to bathe in the waters of the Ganges and in all other rivers of the earth together with other believers. Christians are discovering that these rivers are genuine rivers, though they do not belong to christianity. That constitutes, in spite of some noticeable exceptions in the past, a new sociological situation.

The exceptions deserve brief mention here, because the present focus on dialogue is a *kairological* moment that was not completely absent in older times. We might refer to Minucius Felix, to the disputes in Barcelona and Toledo, to Ramon Llull, to Bernard of Clairvaux, to Nicholas of Cusa, and in recent times to Brahmabandhav Upadhyaya, to John Wu, and to many others. All of them witness to the fact that the need for dialogue as sensed today is not completely new. In addition, there has always been an existential interchange on the more conventional level, where population groups of different religious convictions have lived together. For example, in Kerala, India, members of the religions popular there— namely, hindus, christians, and muslims—have been living together for hundreds of years in a relatively positive symbiosis.

From this historical survey, we should draw some theological conclusions. The *first* lesson to be learned comes from history and the fact that all talking depends on the time element—historical circumstances, that is. If the world had not been decolonized politically, we would not talk the way we do today. Dialogue did not evolve from speculation; instead, it was almost forced on christians because of circumstance. Practice governs theory. However, it also proves wise to make the best of every situation.

The *second* lesson should be one of liberation from both a narrow, one-dimensional supernaturalism and a merely dialectic materialism. The change of christian perspectives is not caused merely by a clairvoyant God leading a certain people, nor is it simply the result of cynical calculation on the part of the institutionalized churches hoping thus to retain power and to control people's coins and consciences. Both factors—and others—might be at work here. But still, historical circumstances force us to form certain perspectives, and that does not preclude the possibility that these circumstances in turn are the result of other forces effective in history. A divine factor also is not impossible, though it certainly is not that of a *deus ex machina*. The spirit of God, to use traditional language, should not be confused with—nor separated from—the spirit of the time (*Zeitgeist*). History explains the *how* but not the *why*. In other words, history teaches that neither the best always win (blessed by divine providence) nor the most clever ("blessed" by mere power). According to the *Bhagavadgītā*, both *Dharmakshetra* and *Kurukshetra* belong together. (By the way, the *Sarasvatī*, the third invisible source of the Ganges whose existence is disputed, leads right through *Kurukshetra*.) In other words, both wheat and weeds grow together.

The *third* lesson invites us to synthesize and ponder the importance of all our findings, including our theological and intellectual achievements. Our critical attitude toward past ideologies shows us that we are no exception and that our ideologies do not fare much better than those of our ancestors. We too have been placed in the limited and ultimately makeshift frame of history. We are just as transitory a phenomenon of time as our ancestors. We have to be careful of *chronocentrism* as much as of *ethnocentrism*.

The *fourth* lesson stresses the creativity and freedom involved in authentic theological thought. Theology does not merely repeat former doctrines or simply draw implicit conclusions from them. It creates new things. Theology's resolutions and insights can have far-reaching effects; they can go a new direction, which is not simply a "processing" of already existing dogma. There are mutations and freedom in the real world. Theology is not only exegesis but also practice. Apart from coming to conclusions, theology also poses new premises and creates new situations. Theology is more than conclusions. In other words, the history of christian self-understanding is not a logical development of premises. It is the result of a series of different factors, many of which are free movements of both the human and the divine spirits. One might say in conclusion: The logical continuity of the previous observations does not furnish the criterion that determines the next step.

Though it may presuppose these observations, the next step is not necessarily contained in them. Life is more than logical development—and more than evolution.

History, too, teaches us the right way to approach our subject. In order to avoid expanding this chapter too much, I shall only sketch the methodological principles involved.

Methodological Principles

1. A christian reflection about christian self-understanding must take into account three aspects:

—the original sources of christian self-understanding;

—the interpretation of these sources within tradition;

—the personal experience of these sources and traditions and a renewed reflection about their significance.

The art of theology consists in blending these three factors to a convincing harmony.

2. A theological interpretation of the christic principle must avoid the following:

—committing apostasy, which means separating oneself from the particular tradition one would like to see advance;

—diluting tradition by wanting to find a common denominator, which ultimately is without shape and form—not even for the sake of tolerance and ecumenical spirit;

—disregarding proper knowledge of other traditions.

Christian self-understanding must be open to other religious experiences and belief-forms (and systems). It must be willing to listen to them, to learn from them, even to absorb all they have to offer that will enrich or deepen the christian interpretation. Christian self-understanding must show willingness for mutual transformation in dialogue. This interreligious enrichment could produce a new ability of perception and ultimately a new form of religious awareness and of religion in general.

3. The method must be dialogical[13] and needs to be applied at the following levels:

—among the various religions, which means in this case between christianity and the other world religions;

—at the heart of one's own religion, which means between the various expressions of christian self-understanding and the various theologies;

—in the soul of theologians themselves or those persons involved in such an undertaking. Dialogue itself is an intimate religious experience.

I shall not elaborate on any of these points since I hope that the chapter itself can be an example of such a methodology.

Three Geo-Theological Moments

Thus far, the nature of the christic principle has been summed up mainly in historical categories, as has also been done in the above analysis of the five *kairological* moments. But it is also, and more properly, transhistorical. The event of the christic principle is neither merely past nor exclusively present. It belongs to the order of the heart, to the personal life of the believer. It is contemporary, *sui generis,* transcending to a certain degree both time and space without deactivating the time-space frame. It is theological in nature. It prompts reflection about what is, both in light of one's own tradition and in light of others' traditions—though everything appears, at any given moment, as if filtered by our own optical equipment. The three geo-theological moments are simultaneously *kairological* in nature. They are intertwined with each other, and each of them is present in the other. Still, each respective moment appears supreme at any of the points in time at which christian conscience manifests itself.

Both history and tradition are *loci theologici* (sources of theological activity). Any contemporary theological reflection that ignores the new context is methodologically faulty. Neither dogma nor christian self-understanding is an a-historical or an a-geographical fact. Geography as much as history constitutes a category both human and religious in nature.

122

While the five facets of christian self-understanding described above are developed along historical lines, the three theological moments described here are to follow a religious-geographical model. If it is true that the way in which the christic principle appeared in the third century differs from that in the twentieth, then there is also a similar difference between the christian experience at the Tiber and that at the Ganges. My metaphor of the river is more than a clever geographic technicality; it is a theological category. Regardless of whether or not christianity is universal, the christian interpretation of life in an african desert is different from that in a scandinavian city. Thus far we have been much more attentive to history than to geography.

We should recognize that the geography of christianity cannot be reduced to the Jordan in Palestine, to the Tiber in Italy, or to the Ganges in India. Not only do fauna and flora vary along the banks of the earth's rivers but also the people and their religious existence. The geo-theological variables are neither cartesian parameters nor neutral geometric ones; they influence the nature of people and their concepts of faith. The "geography of religion" as discipline is still largely unexplored. In addition, geography and history are intertwined.

The Tiber, for example, is not simply the river of Rome. Rome includes also Byzantium, and for centuries Moscow has been the third Rome. Moreover, the italian city itself represents a threefold Rome: the Rome of the Caesars (the christian as well as the non-christian), the Rome of the popes (with or without secular power), and the Rome of the people. Still, I would like to regard the Tiber as a representative of the second area of christian geography. What follows is necessarily only a brief survey.

The Jordan: Water, Faith, Event, Religiosity, Heavenwardness—Exclusivism. Jesus is the Christ. That may be the shortest formula of christian faith. Though the word "Christ" can have many meanings, the origins of this formula are quite closely related to the jewish concept of the Messiah, in spite of the reservations Jesus himself apparently had about this title. In the grammatically synonymous messianic titles "anointed one," "Messiah," "Christos," "Christ," and "Jesus Christ," there occurs a gradual shift of meaning in practical usage.

Christian self-understanding is in an intimate way—both in continuity and in confrontation—connected with the jewish Bible. Circumcision is abolished and this effects a breach with judaism. Yet circumcision is "replaced" by baptism in *water,* which, of course, meant the waters of the Jordan. These waters baptized Jesus, the son of Mary, the Son of Man. They are holy waters because the spirit of God hovered over them (cf. Gen. I:2). Water is a symbol of initiation: it cleanses, it flows, it forms a polarity to fire, it comes from sources and rivers but also from high above and deep below the ground, and, it brings both death and new life. Yet there is only one Jordan. Not everybody is initiated. *Exclusivism* lurks here, although any water can be Jordan water, as we will see later.

The christian is a person of *faith.* This faith has its basis in the person of Jesus. Therefore, theological discussions have to explain who Jesus is. Yet the primary point here is less Jesus' nature than the reality of the *Jesus-event,* especially the event of the resurrection. This event is, above all others, a historical fact in the life of Jesus: the condemnation of one man from Palestine by the judicial religious and lawful authorities of his time. We are here firmly rooted in history and especially in the personal history of Jesus; hence, loyalty to his person is at the center. The teachings of this young rabbi are fascinating, though most of his words may have been expressed by others before him. His example exerts an irresistible magnetism.

To this day, christians are looking heavenward, despite the warning of the angels during the ascension. Christians are maintaining a "religious" attitude, which permeates their lives; it is a very particular "religiosity," not a religion. They are *looking heavenward* to the ascended Christ. Eschatological hopes are prevalent among them. Christ's resurrection will procure and effect "our" resurrection.

It is a privilege to come under the influence, the magic, and the mercy of Jesus. It is something of special importance and bestows a certain dignity; it is a fountain of joy but involves also a burden and a responsibility. The Jordan has a very distinct power—to continue with my metaphor of the river—and jewish writings expressed it. "Are not the Abana and the Parpar, the rivers of Damascus, better than all the rivers of Israel?" Naaman, general of King Aram's army, called out to Elisha, prophet of Israel (II Kings V:12). In other words, uniqueness, privilege, and exclusivism do not constitute an insurmountable problem in a hierarchical world. The number of christians is small, and even smaller is the one of those saved.[14] As long as one is living in a hierarchical context, there is nothing repulsive about a certain amount of exclusivism.

This first moment corresponds to the first historical epoch described above—the epoch of *witnessing*. Through it, one can explain why the central theological problems regarding the "Jordan" are connected with the identity of Jesus Christ, a fact expressed in the christological and trinitarian themes.

The Tiber: Fire, Confession, Institution, Religion, Inwardness— Inclusivism. Is the Jordan, indeed, the only river? Is there not also a way to baptize with fire? Fire burns the old and expands vastly. It cleanses, but it also injures. The present christian identity cannot be limited to the experience of the first generations of christians. One should not overlook the cultural and religious constructs christian life has produced over the past twenty centuries. At this point, we are in the second, third, and fourth epochs, according to the above matrix—*conversion, crusade,* and *mission*—which span fifteen centuries of christian history.

The christian is obliged to hold a certain worldview, expressed in a series of *confessions of faith*. Being a christian does not only mean being loyal to Christ; it also requires membership in the christian community, be it called the church or the world of faith. Splits and schisms, once established, develop their own orthodoxies. Christianity became an *institution*. The feeling of togetherness was highly institutionalized. The ideal was christendom, the christian empire, the christian civilization. When in approximately the sixteenth century this ideal started to disintegrate, it was gradually replaced by the idea of christianity as *religion*.

The Jordan is both a geographical and a mystical river. Its water is baptismal water. The Tiber, on the other hand, is both a historical and a political river. Its water flows into the Thames, the Seine, the Paranâ, and the Potomac. It carries with it a theology, a well-structured worldview, though both broad and flexible. It is the water of both past and present christian civilization. Christendom and its successor, christianity, are not only private matters. Christian waters flow everywhere; they irrigate all fields of a civilization claiming to encompass the whole world. One could assemble a number of contemporary names here—Pope John Paul II, President Bush, Queen Elizabeth, General Pinochet, the philosophers Jacques Maritain and Etienne Gilson, the theologians Karl Barth or Bernard Lonergan, the historians Arnold Toynbee or Friedrich Heer. All these people represent a belief in the superiority of christianity. Although this belief does not prevent one from admitting the greatness of others and the weaknesses of christians, it argues that such confessions are merely made in accordance with christian values and by Christ's authority.

Christianity has become so powerful and universal, so convinced of its mission, that it does not see the necessity of looking outside, unless it wants to learn and become more perfected. Its *inwardness* on mystical, religious, and political levels is one of its characteristics. According to this view, one can find in christian revelation, doctrine, practice, and life-style everything needed for any human life and for the evaluation of other religions and cultures. This is the kind of *inwardness* I have been talking about: it is within ourselves that we find the whole truth. Theology is directed inward. We want to find within ourselves, within our own tradition or revelation, the answer to all theological questions. Although we may talk about others, we may honor them, we may integrate them in our system, it is still *we* who are accomplishing this task. Here is an example: When for the first time in church history an ecumenical council not only acknowledged the right of existence of other religions but even praised them—namely, in *Nostra aetate* of the Second Vatican Council—no one deemed it necessary to invite any representatives of these other religions so that they could speak for themselves. The catholic experts were confident enough in themselves to speak for the others. The Tiber was sufficient.

A heavy theological discourse exists in defense of a certain kind of christian *inclusivism*. The christian religion represents, according to this view, the climax of religious development; it stands for universal values and hence is justified in claiming universality. In short, christianity has no need for despising other religions. It simply stands at the top of a linear evolution. This sort of thinking is often called "fulfillment theology." Christianity is not here the enemy but the fulfillment of all religions.

The following expressions are all indicative of the same syndrome: *Anima naturaliter christiana,* "anonymous christians," "servant of humanity," "kingdom of nature and of mercy"; or, in secular terms, "democracy," "world civilization," "world power," "a world market," "universal human rights," a universally valid science with its own technology. All expressions are saying the same thing: all rivers carry the same water. Yet ultimately it is "our" water, although the canoes going up and down the river may not be aware of it.

There are certainly many institutions, churches, and theologies. Often they wrestle with each other for power, for a better understanding of each other's particular theological questions (on both the internal and ecumenical levels) or for better methods of dealing with other religions. Yet in the midst of these differences we still discover the same kind of language. Could we call it the western *logos*? Christians respond irritably to such a qualification; they say the *logos* is universal (though it only can be "our" *logos*). If not the Tiber itself, its water is everywhere. Therefore, we need *fire* and an *inwardness*.

The attempts for greater open-mindedness within this inclusivist attitude are commendable. Thus, one talks about an invisible christianity, a cosmic Christ,[15] a universal spiritual church, one single God who can make sense also to buddhists, and one law which does not exclude *nomos, dharma, karma,* or *li.* The ideal is a "universal theology of religion" or, in more scientific language, a unified field theory.[16] This kind of Tiber would indeed be longer than the Mississippi.

As long as christianity remains invisible, Christ unknown, the church spiritual, God inexpressible, the law unwritten, and theology unpracticed, there will not be any problems here. *Homo loquens tamen,* "yet the human being remains a talking creature." We cannot utter language as such, just as we cannot practice religion as such. Instead, we have to speak a certain kind of language and practice a certain kind of religion. But then christian universality becomes doubtful and collapses—unless . . . .

It collapses unless one regards the christian phylum as so privileged that it can absorb all others and become a single Amazon for the entire world. That is the case in the many new forms of revival movements and of fundamentalism. With all these phenomena, the focus is on taking care of one's own identity.

It is also clear that the primary theological questions are dependent on who these christians are and what their destination is: questions of ecclesiology, of the doctrine of grace, of salvation, of their relationship to other religions and orthodoxy in general.

The Ganges: Earth, Trust, Religiousness, Measure, Outwardness— Pluralism We are faced now with the challenge of a "theology" for the postcolonial era. This theology corresponds to the attitude of dialogue, described above as the fifth epoch. A dialogical theology insists on its statements only when the discussed matter—and certainly also the language—is recognized as common or created in mutual dialogue. Furthermore, the agenda of the dialogue should be worked out in dialogue itself. In other words, *Gangotri* is only one of the sources of the Ganges, and the delta is no longer only a river, not even an "indian" territory. The snow on the mountains and the clouds in the sky are the sources of *our* Ganges. None of these actually consists of water.

The symbol here is *Earth*. It stands for the *secular (saeculum)*, for the kingdom of justice here on earth, which brings with it the willingness for cooperation with all others, although we might not share their views. There is no such thing as a global consciousness; but there is a special kind of perception of the other and of others, and there is a special kind of willingness that welcomes this consciousness without suffocating it—by accepting it, that is, though one may not understand it. We *trust*. We have a greater trust in our destiny than in the kind of security (certainty) the *logos* provides. Thus, christian identity begins to act less as if it had to defend its own culture, less as if it belonged to an institutionalized religion. Instead, it presents itself as life lived through personal *religiousness*—that is, as a religious attitude, forming one *dimension* of the human being, one factor of the *humanum,* one aspect of the divine.

Then christians will no longer be concerned only with themselves but will also open up to others and to the world as a whole. The *outward* orientation is characteristic of this moment. One goes out not to conquer but to enter into a relationship. It is an attitude that views myself in relation to others and others in relation to myself. I do not call it openness in order to safeguard the balance with the other two moments. An example can perhaps clarify what I mean.

Christian theology of the second moment has been inclined to emphasize the newness of the christian message and to defend its identity by means of differences; it did so by saying that neighborly love, the doctrine of the Trinity, the doctrine of grace, and so on, were specific and unique attributes of christian revelation.[17] Whatever the singular case may be, one feels more comfortable within this third moment, where one discovers that all these doctrines and sayings of various peoples are common property and that it is simply these peoples' primordial and original traditions that christianity has come to embody.

Neither *exclusivism* nor *inclusivism* describes the proper attitude of this third moment. I am talking of *pluralism* here.

Before unfolding the positive aspects of this new moment, which I have termed *christianness*, I should like to review some of its negative traits (which have led us, much like Moses, to the border of the promised land). At their basis lies the possible impossibility of comparing ultimate worldviews.

Dialogue Between a Hindu-Vedantin and a Christian Theologian

Christian: Let us start with our common faith in God.

Hindu: Do you mean *brahman,* absolute reality, underlying everything?

Christian: No, I mean God, the singular, the only one, creator of heaven and earth.

Hindu: Perhaps you are talking about *Îshvara, saguna brahman,* the power and the consciousness of the divine?

Christian: Is that the ultimate, to which thought cannot add anything greater?

Hindu: Yes and no. Yes, insofar as we cannot think with our *manas* anything more ultimate. No, insofar as there is a *jñāna* consciousness of the *nirguna brahman.* And no again, since *thought* of the ultimate by itself cannot be *the* ultimate.

Christian: We should not discuss philosophy here but theology. Or better, we should not criticize concepts of thought but instead try to offer a plausible explanation of our faiths.

Hindu: I am getting confused here. Are you saying perhaps that *shraddhā,* faith, that to which we give our heart (according to etymology), can be reduced to a formula?

Christian: Are you opposed to the endeavor of a *fides quaerens intellectum,* a faith that relies on reason in order to "translate" into intelligible terms what is God's gift or a participation in God's knowledge?

Hindu: And you are saying that is not philosophy? All these concepts you are using need careful explanation. Why do we not start with Christ and presuppose that we are both acknowledging a sphere of *adhidaivika,* which embraces us?

Christian: I would prefer saying it is above us.

Hindu: If the "above us" does not exclude the "among us," we might agree here.

Christian: Christ is the Son of God.

Hindu: I thought we wanted to avoid a premature discussion of the divine.

Christian: Christ is the savior of the entire universe.

Hindu: Who is Christ?

Christian: You asked me to avoid talking about God too soon. Christ is the one, singular mediator between the temporal and the eternal worlds.

Hindu: Two questions: Do we need a mediator? Is Christ the only one?

Christian: We are not, or are not yet, God. Pantheism is the wrong conclusion. We need a connection between both spheres. Christ is the only connection for the same reason that there is only one God: If there were two Gods, they would coalesce.

Hindu: I hope I am understanding all you have been saying so far. After all, I have studied your language. But all of it sounds irrelevant and strange.

Christian: How else would you like me to say it?

Hindu: There is only one reality. We are it, and we are in it. By means of authentic wisdom, *jñāna,* we become what we know, although we were already it before.

Christian: Is this not a contradiction? When you *are* something already, you cannot *become* it later.

Hindu: This is the reason why becoming only appears as such, and it is only becoming from the viewpoint of the one apparently becoming.

Christian: Now we are talking philosophy again.

Hindu: If our words are to make sense, can we really avoid that?

Christian: We could try limiting our conceptual frame to a minimum. Jesus is the son of Mary. He was crucified and was raised on the third day. God raised him from the dead—but we could leave out the divine cause here.

Hindu: That might be a better beginning. The risen Christ means that he is supposed to be our model and we should imitate him. I can agree with that completely. Jesus' life is sublime and inspiring, but there are other examples too.

Christian: Let me say in your language that Jesus was a completely realized person, a human being totally made divine.

Hindu: But this is nothing unique, apart from the fact that everybody is unique.

Christian: He has founded his church as an ark of salvation for all humankind.

Hindu: For one, I do not see the need of founding a church. For another, how about those remaining outside in both the temporal and the spatial senses?

Christian: Could I not say that he did it the way Buddha did in founding the *sangha,* thereby making it easier for the monks to find liberation. There is a simple answer to the second question: Though the church is visible, its borders are invisible.

Hindu: Then the church is merely an institution like many others.

Christian: The moment we decide not to discuss the question of God and, hence, of the Son of God, christian faith has already lost its contours.

Hindu: Why is it, then, that you cannot agree that we all are "children of God"—to say it in your words—and that Christ was one of the oldest, the first-begotten son, if you will?

Christian: There is a difference. He is the lord of history—by way of avoiding further God talk.

Hindu: That either makes no sense, in my opinion, or I have to call it absurd. To us, this philosophical concept of history is foreign, though it appears such a heavy burden to you. The unfolding of linear time is nothing but an illusion and a fragmentation of reality. In referring to the Old Testament, we will have to distinguish between christianity at large and what you call a religion. Christianity does not have a saving effect. It teaches you only to be victorious in history. It is becoming rather suspect, and these twenty centuries of christianity are a good example that my distrust is not too farfetched.

Christian: I have to agree with you here. What you are condemning, christianity itself condemns by its own standards.

Hindu: Does that mean that we are basically agreeing on the ethical level, while our two differing metaphysical concepts prevent us from even seeing whether there is agreement or disagreement between us?

Christian: It is true, indeed, that we are speaking two different languages.

Hindu: I can in good faith recite your entire Nicene Creed and still interpret it radically differently from you.

Christian: Translations are certainly possible, and we can find homeomorphic equivalents. But still, our differences on the doctrinal level cannot be overcome. We could go on talking forever, but we will always reach the point where the different languages become the problem; they represent different worldviews, different ways of thinking, different basic convictions. . . .

* * *

I have often said that comparative philosophy is, strictly speaking, impossible, because the necessary viewpoint from which the comparison is to be made is already part of a certain philosophical mentality.[18] One could say similar things about the study of comparative religion.[19] We cannot presume that all religious traditions can be exactly and truthfully measured by the same *metron* (measuring rod) unless we presuppose that reason (which ultimately is only "our" understanding of reason) is neutral, universal, and a sufficient criterion for evaluating religions. Every religious tradition, as a relatively complete system of self-understanding, develops its parameters from itself. A fruitful dialogue must agree first on the kind of parameters used in this dialogue; otherwise one is simply talking over the other's head. To say it simply, we will have to ask, What is it we mean by the words we use? The discussion concerning the meaning of words precedes the dialogue, thus also determining and forming it.

Its consequence is that religious traditions *can* certainly be incommensurable; it may be that they have no adequate point of being compared with one another. They are, indeed, irreducible, unless an agreement has been reached or constructed. A realistic estimate would, in the current state of affairs, realize that religions, and even theologies, often consider each other as incommensurable.

We should not try to relieve our intellectual frustration by postulating the kind of intellect that can know everything, absolutely everything. Such a hypothesis only pushes aside the real question. It pretends to answer the *why* of being and, by doing so, makes being subject to the *why,* to the *logos,* to consciousness. We could say in the language of logic that an unlimited and supreme intellect embraces everything thinkable. For an unlimited mind there are no boundaries: everything is known to it. Still, we cannot prove in a purely logical manner—unless we identify being with consciousness—that there could not be a kind of being unknown to the supreme intellect.

One might object that such an unlimited intelligence would not be unlimited if it were not able to know everything. We might reply that an unlimited intelligence is unlimited *qua* intelligence, but it is not unlimited *qua* being, assuming, unless we beg the question, that both being and intelligence are ultimately one—and this is the problem. I only indicate that there might be facets of reality that cannot be penetrated by the light of the intellect. I will come back to that when discussing the term pluralism.

While the problems of the two previous moments were of christological-trinitarian nature, on the one hand, and ecclesiological-soteriological, on the other, the theological problems of this moment will depend on the present questions of humankind and the manner in which christians can help to solve them. This does not mean that these problems are merely political, economic, or simply a matter of justice. They are also anthropological, since the human being has reached a particular understanding of itself. And they are also cosmological, which means that they deal with the ideas of the world and of history.

Only when keeping in mind these historical and geo-theological aspects, will we be able to understand the specific challenge and the problems of a pluralistic christian self-understanding in this present time. A few considerations may now be helpful for clarifying our overall problematic.

Three Attitudes: Christendom, Christianity, Christianness

I will begin with the problem of vocabulary. The word "christian" can describe the adjectival content of christendom (of a civilization), of christianity (of a religion), and of christianness (of personal religiousness). During the epoch of the so-called christian culture of the High Middle Ages, one could hardly be a christian without belonging to christendom. And until recently, one could hardly confess to being a christian without belonging to christianity.

Today people have more chance of being christians by maintaining a personal attitude without depending on christendom or christianity with their respective institutional structures. I am talking about a personal, not an individualistic, attitude here. The word "person" always points to community. The christian mentality is *ecclesial* and differs from being *ecclesiastical;* the latter is, in general, synonymous with an enduring, traditional organization. The word *ecclesia* (church) points, strictly speaking, to an organism, not to an organization. An organism needs a soul, a life. An organization requires an idea, a rationale.[20] This distinction is important. Being a christian, being a member of christendom, is largely a matter of the past and of the dreams of a few for the future; but for the majority of christians today it is irrelevant. Still, the spirit and reality of christendom have not disappeared, nor can they be completely eradicated from christian consciousness. It is a part of human nature as well as of christian dynamics to build "sanctuaries" where the christian ideal can become incarnate in the smallest particle of life. In the past, such sanctuaries have been called the christian empire or the christian nation. Later they became religious orders, and today they are sects and new christian movements. All of them are ambiguous—and not completely outdated. Still, the christic principle cannot be sufficiently identified with what we call christendom. There are, in addition, christianity and christianness. There are many rooms in the Father's house!

There is christianity. Being a christian, a member of christianity, means belonging to a religion that is one among many. This religion may be more or less pure than others. Yet it would be not only an abuse of language but a verbal abuse to call the other religions false or to denounce them as nonreligions. The problems of christianity as religion differ from the questions of christendom as a fully grown historical organization.

About one hundred years ago, catholics were excommunicated if they rejected the "divine right" of papal states. Those refuting the right of the church to flog heretics, again, invited excommunication. Today no catholic christian feels obliged any longer to obey the rules, laws, and ordinances of the medieval and renaissance popes. Such obligations belong to christendom, not to christianity.

I would like to add that the papal nuncios, the ambassadors of governments, are still part of christendom, and their function may well be historically justified. Canon law is still valid and papal encyclicals are still of importance—to give a few catholic examples.

But these nuncios and laws no longer exhaust the ways of being a christian, not even those of being catholic.

A third factor emerges powerfully in our time: Viewing oneself as a christian can also mean living a personal faith, taking on a Christlike mentality, and accepting Christ as a symbol of one's personal life. This is what I call *christianness* (spanish *cristianía,* german *Christlichkeit*). It need not be interpreted in exclusively historical terms. It simply exists as a *fact,* as something we discover and simultaneously as something that is not merely found by us. Elsewhere I introduced a similar distinction between christianity, church, and Christ; there I focused on the social aspect of religion, its sacramental dimension, and its mystical center.[21] The latter might also be called the christic principle.

For clarification, I shall mention a few examples from the roman catholic tradition: The use of contraceptives is formally prohibited by the highest authority of catholic christianity. Still, many members of the catholic church ignore this ordinance and still consider themselves "good catholics." A similar situation is evolving at this point in some countries regarding divorce. In addition, there are more than one hundred thousand properly ordained priests who understand themselves as such, though they have broken what they call the unfair ordinance of celibacy. Abortion, euthanasia, pacifism, capitalism, and communism are similarly conflict-laden issues. Can someone be a communist and still be a christian or be a capitalist and follow the Gospel?

In short, christianness becomes distinguishable from christianity, just as christianity freed itself from christendom. The transition is certainly fluid. Every epoch is one of transition; but there are times when differing traits in respect to the former epoch are particularly conspicuous.

Another example is the South and Central American grassroots communities (*comunidades de base*) as they have spontaneously developed a christianness that is not clearly reflected in traditional christianity. The Vatican has seen that clearly. But institutionalized christianity shows enough theological discrimination, common sense, or political prudence to know that it must not alienate itself from one of the largest christian continents. Hence, it comes up with a political compromise in order to keep christendom, christianity, and christianness together. The christianness of the past century was mainly pietistic and individualistic. It could get along with institutionalized christianity with little difficulty. Present christianness shows an increasingly personal and political engagement and becomes, as such, a challenge to official christianity. Here, as elsewhere, wise is the one who transforms destructive tensions into creative polarities.

Christianness should not be described merely in its negative relation to christianity. I have already said that all three belong together and cannot be completely separated from each other, though they have to be distinguished.

There is also a theological reason for this distinction. Many religions have writings on sacred law. In the two monotheistic religions of Abrahamic origin (judaism, islam), the law is part of revelation itself (Torah, Qur'ân). One might note with irony at this point that Marxism as a fourth Abrahamic religion showed a similar respect for the Communist Party, a respect that could be described as secular revelation. Christianity is different at this point. Christianity does not have its own law. For several centuries, only the "Old Testament" was christianity's Scripture. The "New Testament" was not considered the Bible.[22] Furthermore, christianity does not have a proper name for the highest being. "God" is a *nomen commune*, a "common name." (Jesus called this being "my father," and nothing prevents us from calling it also "mother.") All this speaks for the fact that some kind of christianness is possible that differs from christendom and christianity.

We must emphasize that the mystics living in christendom stood up for christianness at all times. Though the mystics of christianity always showed their respect for the legal superstructures, they did not allow the latter to take them captive. Revolt and dropping out are not christian solutions. Jesus' example comes vividly to mind. He is a denouncer and a protestor, even a transgressor; but he is not a defector, not a traitor. Peter had learned to obey God more than people; yet still he did not want to do away with circumcision— although he accepted being overruled on that by his brothers in the faith and by the Holy Spirit.

When looking back in history, we find, indeed, a number of christians who experienced christianness after they had overcome, yet not discarded, both christendom and christianity. Many simple and strong believers could be mentioned here as examples, but also believers such as Tertullian, Origen, Eckhart, Savonarola, Dante, Vico, Joachim de Fiore, Joan of Arc, John of the Cross, Erasmus, Kant, Hegel; and in our own times Teilhard de Chardin and Pater Pio, Thomas Merton, and Svami Abhishiktānanda.

In summary, the differing interpretations of the Gospel injunction "Look first for the kingdom of God and its justice" (Matt. VI:33) could serve as a guidepost for expressing this threefold structure of christian self-understanding. The first interpretation sees, based on the well-known passage in Luke XVII:21, "the kingdom" as something "among us." The kingdom is, hence, also on earth and has its political implications. The second interpretation underlines the same greek particle, *entos,* and views it as the kingdom "between" us, thereby stressing the cultural-communal aspect. The third interpretation is inclined to regard the kingdom as "within us" and emphasizes the dimension of inwardness. One might say similar things about the interpretation of the word *dikaiosynē*. It can be viewed as political justice, as a doctrinal symbol or as an immanent reality. (In fact, the word *dikaiosynē* in the New Testament means both justice and justification [righteousness].)

The sociological effects of these distinctions are important. In today's world, christian identity doubtless is in crisis. Although revival movements exist that are based on the ideal of a modernized christendom, as well as other movements stressing the more theological tendencies and striving for a reformed christianity, a growing number of responsible people are fighting for the articulation of a genuine christian confession that is fully governed neither by the historical burden of the past nor by the doctrinal narrowness of tradition. They do not actually espouse a privatization of christian identity, though they may almost be forced to do so. Instead, they espouse an exposing of their christian identity, since the latter is a fruit more of their internal experience than of their historical and doctrinal insistence. They are more or less aware that the world is in the process of changing, and they try to live this change in its innermost manifestation—that is, on the religious levels of their consciousness and their conscience.

To say it in simpler words, a considerable number of today's christians want to be religious, pious, and even christian—but without the "contaminations" that, in their view, go with these adjectives. They want to retrieve their roots so they can grow in fresh ground and not be spoiled by the trash of old times, by the parasites of the Middle Ages, by the pesticides of recent times, and by the radiation of modernity. This struggle for reform is innate in the human being; it has always been that way but today assumes cosmic proportions.

Let us draw some explicit connecting lines between these attitudes and our three rivers: If the spirituality of the Jordan is closely related to christianity and that of the Tiber to christendom, then the Ganges is here a symbol of christianness—although all these metaphors should be understood in light of Pascal's *esprit de finesse* (and not *de géometrie*).[23] The Ganges, in fact, since time immemorial has been the symbol not of political or even intellectual power (christendom and christianity) but of personal experience—and experience is paramount in christianness. Except for a very few spots in the mountains, the Ganges is not a spectacular river. Once she leaves the Himalayas she flows smoothly of herself, since she runs for well over a thousand miles almost at sea level. Your sins will be forgiven if you die in her arms with faith. She has no power, but she is endowed with an immense authority—up to purifying the believers of their sins. The original Ganges was in the heavens and came down to earth through the hair of Shiva's head so as not to harm anybody, but she goes further, to the nether world, near her mouth by the island of Sagar. The experience of the three realms is essential to christianness. But as has been already said, Mā Gaṅgā here stands for any other river carrying what until now were supposed to be non-christian waters.

I want to make clear that these three attitudes are just symbols of the complex christic principle of the present. Moreover, the growing awareness of christianness offers a platform by which one might solve the dilemma of exclusivism and inclusivism in favor of a healthy pluralism of religions. It is a pluralism that does not dilute the particular contributions of each individual human tradition.

Three Problems

Concrete and Universal Versus Particular and General. We must distinguish between concreteness and particularity, between universality and generality. The concrete can be universal but the particular cannot. Something is concrete (my faith, my parents, my home) for the very reason that it represents the universal (faith, parentage, homeland). The universal is universal for the reason that it presents the entire field, not because it excludes—as the general does—the concrete. The universal is centered; it faces one's center—*universus,* facing the one. It is incarnate in the concrete.

The christian mentality is concrete, and it should be. It is limited, yet still it represents the whole. As in the mystery of the incarnation, in the concreteness of one person lives the fulness of the divine. I have called this phenomenon the *pars-pro-toto* effect (that is, the part standing for the whole). We see the whole through our windows; we see and are at the same time the whole in part, *totum in parte.*[24] The concrete is *pars pro toto.* The particular, on the other hand, is *pars in toto* (the part in the whole). We *can* "sacrifice" the particular for the sake of the whole, but the concrete we cannot sacrifice.

Our modern geometric mentality interprets the universal as the sum total of parts bordering on each other in order to form a basic geometrical area. According to such a view, one part, a sector of a circle, cannot form the whole. But this is not the traditional way of understanding universality. In christian history, Augustine still translates "catholic," *kat' holon,* literally, *secundum totum,* "according to the whole,"—a religiousness that is complete in our eyes since it contains all we need for our fulfillment and salvation. Only in the wake of the geographical expansion of the late and already declining christendom, did the idea develop that "christianity" in the sense of catholic religion meant the expansion of one single religion over the entire Earth.

Yet there is something else. The word "universal" need not be understood exclusively in a quantitative fashion. One drop of water may resemble another one, yet it is not the other. Both differ numerically and factually. They may contain the exact same amount of water, yet one drop is not the other. Both consist of water, but we would not distinguish them unless the surface tension were to make two drops in space and time. Still, the particular water in one drop is not the other. But when abstracting from the quantity of water (looking from the inside out, so to speak), both are merely water, undistinguishable water. In other words, the water of each drop—not the drops of water—is both concrete and universal. It is both *this* water and simply water.[25] Christian scholastics occasionally mentioned the mirror nature of the universe in the sense that all beings, especially humans, being images and likenesses of God, reflect, mirror, and represent all of reality.

These distinctions have christological effects. Christ as the second Adam represents all of humanity and, in a certain sense, the entire cosmos. That is what the christian tradition according to Paul says. *Minutis minuendis* (in a smaller yet corresponding way), every person represents and symbolizes all of reality. The mechanistic worldview, so prevalent in our time, is a great obstacle in our endeavor to reactivate this liberating insight. The problem of Christ's universality and of christian salvation could be solved in a practical way by viewing it in light of traditional cosmology. It is not a matter of comparing, for example, Christ with Buddha, Krishna, or another figure. It also is not a matter of separate areas of domain. As long as christian theology is operating from the perspective of christendom or christianity, such problems will emerge. But christian theology today can no longer afford to ignore christianness. From the perspective of christianness, the problem is not one of jurisdiction. Doctrines may differ; theologies may disagree with each other; institutionalized religions may negotiate over their areas of influence; but the existential problem of human "salvation" does not consist in who has the proper passport to heaven or which embassy has the right to issue such documents. What we have to change is the very perspective of this question.

In this context, the universality of Christ would present Christ's transparency and perfection. We reach here another cosmology, one dissolving the problem of singularity and universality.[26] We should not confuse Christ's individuality with our individuation of his person; his identity is not his identification (as found by us).[27] Christ is unique, just as any loved child is unique to her parents—*eminenter* (on the highest level), I would add.

Perhaps another example can help. The ptolemaic concept of the solar system was quite complicated. One of the advantages of the copernican revolution was that the new heliocentric system was much simpler than the old. In one stroke, a gigantic number of calculations became superfluous. I am concerned with something similar here. As long as we maintain a mechano-centric concept and a geometrical idea of reality, we will encounter a variety of utterly complicated and hardly solvable problems. Christians can either "cling" to their "Christ" and become exclusivist, or they can give up their claims, dilute their belief, and become inclusivist at best. These two horns of the dilemma are equally unacceptable. The parallel with the copernican revolution consists in transplanting the center of linear history into a *theanthropocosmic* vision, into a trinitarian notion not only of the deity but also of reality.[28] The vision's center is neither the earth (our particular religion) nor the sun (God, the transcendence, the absolute). Instead, each solar system has its own center, and each galaxy rotates around the other. There is no absolute center. Reality itself is concentric since every creature (every tradition) constitutes the center of the universe—of its own universe, to start with. The *theanthropocosmic* view (which sees the unity of the divine, the human, and the cosmos) proposes a kind of trinitarian dynamic where everything is contained in everything else (each person represents the community, and each tradition reflects, corrects, complements, and challenges the other).

Mythos *and* Logos. The changes of the past centuries in cosmology have led to one of the biggest crises in the self-understanding of christian theology. As I have said many times, Cardinal Bellarmine was ultimately right in the dispute with Galileo. Scientific research has to be free, without a doubt, but it can never be severed from theology. Without theology, cosmology loses its goal, its direction; and without cosmology, theology loses its vehicle, its language. Most of the apparently theological difficulties of the present are in reality cosmological problems.

A few examples may suffice: First, there is the resurrection. In a traditional cosmic worldview, the possibility, the plausibility, even the fact of the resurrection does not involve any major problems.

Spontaneous generation was a matter of direct observation; the penetrating of particles in their different layers was a matter of course; miracles did not need to have natural laws suspended; and so forth. The difficulty arises with the post-newtonian worldview and the post-cartesian concept of space and time, of matter and spirit. Words such as heaven, hell, resurrection, and most other christian symbols become undermined and lose their meaning when the cosmology is missing that undergirds these symbols. By simply continuing to theologize along the old lines as if nothing new had happened in the meantime, one creates theological impasses.

Today's discussion concerning the virgin birth is another powerful example of this problem. The traditional tenet of the virgin birth has nothing to do with the physiological functions of the body understood in cartesian terms. The tenet has a very old cosmological and mythical pedigree and is directly related to the saving function of Jesus. In this traditional worldview, Christ could be a divine redeemer only if devoid of original sin. And people believed that original sin was transmitted by human semen. *Ergo* . . . .

In short, *christian* self-understanding is not independent from the *human* worldview, and the latter has changed. I am not saying that we know better now and have the correct understanding of the world, that alchemy is wrong and chemistry is right, that astrology is superstition and astronomy is science. I am simply uncovering a change in cosmology, which affects all problems and issues of theology.

One should emphasize here that most of the present theological efforts in this area accept the predominant cosmological worldview as given and try reformulating theological insights within these parameters in a new way. That is a noble undertaking and literally necessary for those that have absolutized the modern scientific paradigm: for the disciples of Galileo Galilei! Typical examples of it are the disputes on the Eucharist and the doctrine of creation in the theological schools of some countries. The doctrines of transubstantiation and of creation *ex nihilo* (out of nothing) do not make sense in a molecular and evolutionist worldview. I do not agree with the literal and fundamentalist interpretations, but I would like to relativize in similar fashion the basic cosmological perspectives of modern science. The Earth is moving, but so is the sun. The aristotelian category of substance may not be a basis for explaining the Eucharist in our present time, but neither are, if not even less so, the theories that speak of a mere transformation of the interpretative meaning. What we lack is *a proper cosmology*.

In summary, one might say that christian self-understanding is neither autonomous nor heteronomous in relation to its cosmological foundations. We must figure out their *ontonomous* relationship to each other.[29] It is not that science dictates what theology is to do, or vice versa.[30] But the fact remains that we cannot do theology without cosmology; neither can we do cosmology without theology. A cosmology without theology becomes itself theological—that is, ultimate. After all, every kind of cosmology says something about our world; from our common destiny with the world, in particular, arises the theological problem. Conversely, a theology without a cosmology becomes devoid of meaning, unless the former transforms itself into a cosmology altogether. After all, every theology says something about the concrete person, whose place in the world cosmology examines and describes. Even an apophatic theology rests on the meanings of words relevant to our cosmos, though it negates these meanings. In other words, this theology is based on the overcoming of a certain kind of cosmology on which it, after all, depends. And even the kind of science purely structured along mathematical lines describes theoretical modes of behavior that have something to do with our lives and, hence, with a theological question.

This fact is of paramount importance, in my opinion. The present crisis stems not from a conflict of differing cosmologies but from a lack of cosmologies. The viewpoint of science is, strictly speaking, no true cosmology. It is only the popularizers that equate science with scientism. Scientists themselves emphasize again and again the limits of scientific endeavors, and they are fully aware of the purely quantitative parameters of science. Yet neither is the scientist as a person able to live in empty space, nor can science itself operate without a world. Similarly, neither can theologians manage without cosmology and limit themselves to exegesis or hermeneutics, nor can theology conjure up theories about a nonreal world.

In a word, neither science nor theology can function well in a cosmological vacuum. Electrons may be but energy quanta, which can be located by a Geiger counter; angels may be merely species by themselves of purely intellectual nature; but we must assign them a place in a coherent or, at least, consistent and existential universe of discourse in order to make them usefully intelligible to human life. Yet without a presupposed cosmology we cannot find a proper "place" for electrons and angels. Hence, the following happens: We extrapolate certain data and "place" both electrons and angels amidst the ruins of a past cosmology. In our predominantly scientific culture, we think it easier to categorize electrons (we call them small energy entities) than angels (we could call them strange energy clots, at best). But in both instances, neither angels nor electrons can reach a proper degree of reality unless they have been integrated in their respective proper universe. At this point, we do not have such a universe—though scientists are trying (perhaps more than philosophers) to construct one.[31]

I am convinced of three things: First, we cannot construct a worldview simply of our liking. Such a worldview must be the spontaneous creation of poets and artists, since it requires inspiration much more than mere logical planning and calculating. Second, it will require our cross-cultural cooperation.[32] The worldview must be the result of a mutual enrichment among cultures and religions. Third, the modern christian consciousness must become sufficiently aware of this cosmological dilemma. Then it no longer can continue reciting uncritically the Nicene Creed, for example, which belongs to a completely different cosmology.[33]

But we should not imagine that we can drink without a container or that we can rid ourselves of all structures—and substructures. It is *one* thing that christians no longer can identify with the Nicene Creed since its formulations have become severed from their proper soil; but it is *another* to think that we can completely demythologize ourselves.[34] We can only "remythologize," surrounding ourselves with different myths, changing them and our view of them. Many metaphysical systems may not be convincing, but we should not repress the search for an explanation of the *physis*. This is what metaphysics is all about.

The correlation between *mythos* and *logos* is a constitutive one.[35]

One cannot exist without the other. Our cosmological background is not independent of the *mythos;* likewise, neither science nor theology can exist without a mythical basis.

These reflections are directly related to our central problem. They tell us that no single intellectual paradigm will ever be sufficient to explain reality, ultimately because reality cannot be reduced to paradigms. These reflections also tell us that our own situation is only a new moment in the adventure of reality. They show us that consciousness, even absolute consciousness, is not everything there is "in" reality. Moreover, these reflections can help us overcome the dialectic impasse of our time in the areas of religion, theology, and science; they make us aware that the problem of truth and reality can never be solved by itself since we are necessarily a part of them. It may be possible for us to objectify a part of reality, but we can never objectify it completely. Otherwise we would eliminate ourselves. This is the level where a discussion of pluralism has its adequate place.

Plurality and Pluralism. The time has come for a *pluralistic attitude*—for a head-first dive into the Ganges.[36] This attitude will be summarized in the following points:

1. Pluralism means neither plurality, or multiplicity, nor a reduction of this multiplicity for unity's sake. It is a fact that there are many religions. It is also a fact that these religions cannot be reduced to some kind of unity. Pluralism means more than mere acknowledgment of this plurality, more than purely wishful uniform thinking.

2. Pluralism does not regard unity as an indispensable ideal, even if variations within this unity were to be acceptable. Pluralism accepts the irreconcilable aspects of religions or world myths without being blind to possible common aspects. Pluralism is not the eschatological expectation that in the end everything will come to unity by itself.

3. Pluralism contends neither that truth is singular nor that there are many truths. If truth were only singular, we could not accept the positive tolerance of a pluralistic attitude and would have to assume that pluralism allows error. If there were many truths, we would become trapped in plain contradictions. We have already said that pluralism does not stand for multiplicity—in this case, for the multiplicity of truth. Pluralism develops a nondualist, *advaitic* attitude,

which defends truth's pluralism since truth itself is pluralistic; that is, it cannot be expressed in terms of unity or multiplicity. Being as such need not be reduced to consciousness, even if being is "embraced" by the *logos* or is "coexistent" with it or with the Highest Intelligence. The perfect mirror image of being is truth; but even if the perfect image of being is identical with truth, being is not exhausted in this image. If the *logos* constitutes the transparency of being, then the spirit is paradoxically its intransparency. The spirit is freedom; it is the freedom of being to be what it is. And that cannot be anticipated by the *logos* in an a priori fashion. The *logos* accompanies being; it does not precede it, does not prescribe what being is. It simply says what being is. The *being* of being is free. The mystery of the Trinity is the ultimate ground for pluralism.

4. Pluralism has no room for a universal system. A pluralistic system would be a contradiction in itself. The incommensurability of ultimate systems cannot be overcome by the *logos*. This incommensurability is not a pesky evil (that would mean that one forms opinions only on account of the *logos*) but a primordial revelation of reality's nature. There is nothing that reality itself could embrace.

5. Pluralism makes us aware of our contingency, our limitations, and it shows us that reality cannot be fully comprehended. Pluralism cannot be matched up with the monotheistic assumption that there is a totally intelligible person—an omniscient consciousness that is identical with being. Still, pluralism does not shrink back from the dimension of intelligibility. A pluralistic attitude attempts, as far as possible, to penetrate this dimension, but it does not need the ideal of a completely thinkable reality. It "knows" that we have to stop somewhere in order to keep from destroying being (the "originality" or independence of being) by reducing it to mere thinkability even if it were self-intelligibility.

6. Pluralism is, hence, a mere symbol. It has an attitude of cosmic trust (in the spirit, which is not subordinated to the *logos*), which permits a polar and tension-filled coexistence of *ultimate* human convictions, cosmologies, and religions. It neither eliminates nor absolutizes evil or error.

7. Pluralism does not deny the *logos* and the *logos*'s proper rights. The principle of noncontradiction, for example, cannot be eliminated. But pluralism also belongs to the sphere of the *mythos*. It

embodies the *mythos*—of course, not as an object of thinking but as the horizon that ultimately makes thinking possible. The *mythos* is the seat of belief.

In view of this description of pluralism, a christian pluralistic attitude would have the following tenets:

1. There is no single christian self-understanding.

2. Self-understandings are many.

3. They cannot be brought together under one common denominator or one supersystem. (These first three tenets are simple facts; even the third can hardly be denied. From these result the following characteristics of christian pluralism.)

4. Differing theologies should be regarded as christian if they call themselves that. The unity of christian theology is beyond logical reasoning and power of judgment, since it is quite likely that one theology considers another as incompatible with basic christian belief, yet they still claim to be christian. Hence, although such theologies are existentially connected as christian, they may not have a common denominator, a common essence, on a theological level. The existential criterion of belonging together does not eliminate the diversity of their respective *logoi*. After all, it could happen *any time* that several theologies find a common denominator, not detected previously.

Although one might be able to formulate, based on some tenets, a foundation common to all christian theologies, none of these theologies would thereby be sufficiently described. (That is also true for the currently dominant theology of the "west," which forgets its own historical multiplicity with its claim to universality in faith matters.) The inner coherence of a theological system makes minimal "truths" dependent on the system's overall representation in the total picture. Insofar as these total pictures differ, the apparently common denominator is a mere reductionist abstraction. All christian theologies may, for example, acknowledge "Christ's central role," but the meaning of this phrase—and even the context—may differ vastly.

5. We should not prescribe, based on a single perspective, what other christian perspectives ought to be. This would result in introducing ourselves as the ultimate criterion for christian identity; it would destroy pluralism. Pluralism belongs to the sphere of the *mythos*.

6. A christian pluralistic attitude must be willing to become excommunicated by a nonpluralistic viewpoint without then wanting to take revenge in judging the other as non-christian. Pluralism undermines the arguments for a power struggle.

7. Christian pluralism could assume as its motto the phrase "All that is not against us is for us." Whatever does not contradict a concrete opinion cannot be refuted. However, each reply carries with it also the limits within which it is valid. It is never absolute. The principle of tolerance should rest not on acknowledging truth but on having trust.

8. A christian pluralistic attitude should cling to christian tenets when facing other world religions without forgetting the limitation and contingency of the particular subject that is formulating them. It would not announce, for example, that "X is the true faith." Rather, it would confess that "I believe that X is true [the true faith]." The content of faith should never be severed from this "I believe." Still, one can express the conviction that others are not correct, even that their views are harmful. One can sense the obligation to fight individual wrong conceptions. Yet one should never regard these as absolute evils, and one should keep in mind the limitations of one's own power of judgment.

9. A pluralistic christian will not confess many saviors. That would be a nonpluralistic assertion, since the faith experience of the savior is unique for each believer and cannot be multiplied. A pluralistic christology will begin by saying that the mystery of Christ cannot be reduced to a quantitative understanding: While believing that the mystery of Christ is of far-reaching significance, I cannot possibly say that it is only important to my own personal salvation, my own church, or my church's doctrinal tradition. Yet it would be improper to absolutize my own limited understanding in such a way that I monopolize this mystery. Equally impudent is the presumption that all savior figures of religious history are in reality the christian Christ only with different names. How could I know? The doctrine of the Trinity in Christian tradition warns of such quantifications. Augustine said regarding the Trinity: *Qui incipit numerare, incipit errare* ("whoever starts counting, starts erring"). The saving power—which christians call Christ—is neither simply one nor many.

Therefore, christian self-understanding is a function of the all-embracing *mythos,* which prevails at a certain time in a certain place. This unifying *mythos* may not be a constant, and it may not be equally present at all times. The *mythemes* valid for the present situation will now be summarized in a few concluding points.

Conclusions

A christian reflection concerning religious pluralism and its implications can incorporate the following points in its program:

1. We should not ignore the past or neglect it; we should respect traditional self-understandings yet subject them to appropriate (new) interpretations.

2. We should not be satisfied with purely exegetical ways of access if the former absolutize the fixed contents of tradition. After all, christian self-understanding does not consist only of hermeneutics. We should consider the possibility of a new christian consciousness.

3. The most important change in christian self-understanding relates both to text and to context. The text is expanded if one incorporates other sacred texts, excluded so far. In other words, a reflection on the "christian economy of salvation" cannot ignore the existence—and the challenge—of world religions. The traditional christian context was symbolized by the Tiber. The Ganges is the new context—that is, not the context of western history but the *mythos* of the present time. The Ganges here certainly does not mean the exclusively hindu river (so to speak, a Jordan of hinduism), but it is a symbol of the many rivers of the world.

4. The new context is not simply a new territory added to the old; it is not the same territory viewed in a new light. The new context not only introduces many new elements that were previously nonexistent; it also transforms the old context. It forms a new connection which embraces the old, corrects, and supersedes it, yet still maintains a continuity with it. Still, the new context is limited and concrete as much as the old. It should not be regarded as a universal system; that would ultimately lead to an antipluralistic homogenizing of the world.

5. We should not identify the christic principle, as expressed in *christianness,* with *christianity* as a religion—and much less with *christendom* as a civilization.

6. There is no single way of viewing Christ, no matter how broad it may be. No single view can embrace the reality of Christ.

7. Religions may be incommensurable—apart from a few common traits. Every religion is unique, just as every creature. But we should not confuse the autopsy of religion with its living existence. This incommensurability, like that of the radius and the circumference, does not preclude that every religion can be a dimension of the other in a kind of trinitarian *perichôrêsis* or *circumincessio*. Every religion represents the whole of human experience in a concrete way.

8. Every religion expresses a concrete form of humanness. This does not exclude a possible divine influence on the *humanum;* neither does it exclude a possible religious aberration.

9. When religions come face to face, they can enrich but also destroy each other.

10. If christians are able to liberate the christic principle from their religion, christianity, then this principle can be experienced as a dimension that is at least potentially present in every human being, assuming that no absolute interpretation is added to it. One could say the same about similar principles in other traditions (buddhism, for example).

11. Christians may discover in this christic principle the key to unity, to understanding and love for all humankind, and to the whole of the cosmos, so they can behold in this concreteness the most radical human, cosmic, and divine communion with reality—regardless of other possible homeomorphic equivalents.

12. The christian starting point is the kenotic experience of Christ (the experience of Christ's self-emptying to become human), which involves the acceptance of, and openness to, the Spirit.

In conclusion one can say that being aware of the comprehensive context of our world today leads us to realize that christian self-understanding has changed. This change is conditioned by the following factors: (1) *Historical changes:* the transition of christendom to christianity and, moreover, to the christian attitude expressed in christianness. (2) *The philosophical distinctions* between the concrete/particular and the universal/general—the overcoming of quantitative patterns of thinking. (3) *Cosmological revolution:* the worldview in which christianity grew up no longer is able to withstand critical scrutiny. (4) *The theological recognition* of the rights and values of other religions, resulting in a healthy pluralism.

All this both presupposes and simultaneously causes our deep and conscious insight into the basic christic principle. Through this awareness, social and religious structures of history can be transcended.[37] We are slowly recognizing the necessity of a new christian awareness, which is tied neither to christian (western) civilization nor to christian (institutionalized) religion. New communities could spring up, even in traditionally non-christian countries, and some of them may even avoid the name "christian" since the label "christian" could be understood as a *mere* continuation of the past.

The point is not to deny the civilization-related christian aspects or to lessen the importance of organized religion. The point is simply to emphasize one's personal spiritual life, one's discovery of the heavenly kingdom, of the pearl, of the totality of the mystical body, of the union with the divine, of the internal, of the historic, and at the same time of the cosmic and transhistorical Christ. There were times when it was dangerous to be a christian and times when it was advantageous. Both possibilities are real even today. Yet I would like to emphasize a third trait: It is difficult to be a christian. It is difficult today because it requires personal discipline, the courage of facing not only the secular world but also ecclesiastical institutions. Christianness stands for the experience of Christ's life in us, for the insight that we are in communion with all of reality without losing our identity; it stands for the experience that "I and the Father are one," that labels are not relevant, that certainty is hardly important, that even reflection is only a secondary source of knowledge (though a primary tool). Only hesitantly am I using here the phrase "mystical experience"; but there is perhaps no better expression. I had good reasons for choosing the mystical Ganges as a symbol. Does it not relate to what Christ said when referring to the "waters of eternal life" (John IV:14)—waters from any river or ocean? One only has to drink them.

The Cosmotheandric Christ

I will end this reflection on a personal note, which may cast a different light on the present analysis. I shall try to indicate my interpretation of Christ from a *theanthropocosmic* viewpoint. I believe that this interpretation follows the methodological principles of this chapter; yet I should not recommend in any way considering it as normative or necessarily representative for christian theology.

The mystery which is the beginning and will be the end; the Alpha and the Omega through which everything comes into being; the light shining upon all creatures; the word contained in every authentic word; reality entirely material, completely human, and simply divine yet everywhere at work and unreachably present wherever reality exists; the meeting place at the crossroads of reality where all kingdoms meet; that which does not come with trumpet sounds and which one should not regard as being here or there; that of which we are not aware when acting in good or bad ways and which is still "right there"; that which we are—and are supposed to be—and which we have been; this symbol of all reality, not just as it used to be or is now but also as it will continue to be freely, even through our cooperation; that mystery, I believe, is Christ. In case someone says that this symbol is too broad and universal, I shall reply: Since the circumcision of the body has been done away with, why not also do away with that of the mind?

With such a view of Christ I am not avoiding the *skandalon* of the Incarnation and the process of salvation. I am not ignoring these facts. The point is simply that I am not worshiping history as if it were God, and I am not limiting reality to history—not even to human history—and not to the history of abrahamic lineage. Just as traditional theology speaks of a *creatio continua,* we might imagine, analogously, a continued incarnation, not simply in the body but also in the actions and events of all creatures. Every creature is a *christophany*.

"This Is You"
Questions and Answers in Summary

This summary is an adventure in summarizing summaries. At the same time, it is a synthesis of something whose mastery would take a long time. It is also a condensation of human life, an image of humanity's destiny, an *anakephalaiōsis,* a recapitulation of the universe's destiny—hence, an extremely high potency!

I would like to summarize, once again, in simple terms, relating my remarks both to the Bible and to the wisdom of the *Upanishads:* The Bible says that the human being was created in the image (*eikôn*) and likeness (*homoiôsis*) of God (Gen. I:26). This means that Man is similar to God; we are of God's race, as the Greeks maintained and as Paul would repeat in agreement (Acts XVII:28). It means further that Man is a mirror of all of creation; that the human being is not only a microcosm but also an image of the macrocosmos, of the entire reality; that in every human being both God's and the World's destinies are reflected. This is the unlimited, even divine, dignity of Man, in whom all dimensions of reality meet.

We have said that the point is to discover the deepest core of being. Yet being does not exist: it is an abstraction—living nowhere, being nowhere, and not to be found. Being as such does not exist; only the idea of being does. Certainly there are many books dealing with the problem of being. But the term "being," by which we attempt to describe reality, is an abstraction, whereas reality itself is not abstract but always concrete. Reality is the "I *am*," the "you *are*," the "it *is*." Hence, what exists is not the being but the "am," "are," "is": the chair is; you are; I am.

At first glance it appears as if the human being is able to think the "is," to feel the "are," to experience the "am." One finds here again a trinity, a trifoldness of the "is," the "are," and the "am," which represents the three dimensions of reality. But what "I" really "am," or what "we" indeed "are," is not too easily determined. If in our search we are chasing the "Who am I?" we will find out that the questioner always retreats, only leaving behind an object, a trace, a *vestigium,* footprints. The I that we are looking for is not me. The I that I eventually find is always the found one; actually it is a You. . . .

The phrase *tat tvam asi* would represent another possibility of expressing this insight: "This you are" (CU VI,8–16). The "You" is mine, my you, and not a "something" it is, or I assume to be. I am a "You." The phrase does not say "I am *brahman*" but "[*tat*] *tvam asi,*" "[this] you are!"

Certainly this "are" cannot be completely separated, and is not independent, from the "am" and the "is." When experiencing myself as the "are," I experience, on the one hand, my essence—which is the deepest there is; on the other hand, I am thereby including the "am," without which the "are" makes no sense and, at the same time, the "is," without which the "are" cannot exist.

I have explained that it is permissible for us to say "I am," "I am the truth." But the "I" enabling me to say so, occurs in a "You." After all, "I am" because "you are." (Here, we are suffering from the deficiencies of our language. There are other languages that do not use the verb "being" in such a way; it would be superfluous to them. Perhaps it is easier for those languages to express this trifoldness.)

Once we are well-grounded in this consciousness, we attain the communion with self, with the entire outside world, with each other, and with the divine. After all, my identity is an "are"; and this "are" only exists in a "you," pronounced by the "I" and based on the "it." This truth could possibly be summed up in the unique formula *tat tvam asi.* One will have to press it quite a bit—but good wine may come from it, and that is my hope!

What kind of meditation would you recommend to the one searching? Zen, yoga, new and traditional forms of christian contemplation, Meister Eckhart, Teresa of Avila, John of the Cross—what do you recommend?

"Pilgrim, there is no path; you yourself are making it by walking!" The hindu term *svadharma* could possibly help here. There are paths, techniques so to speak, which are appropriate for a person or for a certain time; and, by the same token, it would be disastrous to pursue them once the time has passed or to force other people to use them. Thus, a road sign, a master, a guru, a role model in the form of a real-life person may occasionally be helpful as an aid or inspiration from the outside (though we always have to take heed lest obedience and discipline go blind).

The question is quite justified. What one senses in this region of the world is the necessity for a genuine form of meditation and, at times, also the difficulty of walking this path all by oneself. The only thing is, in my opinion, to definitely walk the path. Perhaps one trips and falls when doing so, or one has to take detours; but there is a kind of providence, a *karma,* a coincidence, a cosmic solidarity. Once we open ourselves to it, the proper mentor emerges, if needed. Therefore, I do not have a method, a technique I could recommend. I believe that all techniques are useful and that all of them are obstacles as well. Growth consists primarily in the fact that what used to be the best at the beginning, the middle, or the end of my life, becomes an obstacle. What was very helpful to the novice or during the middle of one's life, may reach the point where it no longer is so. It is like a scaffold, like a pair of crutches, quite appropriate at particular times but not the real thing.

I have given myself nine rules, or *sūtras:*

1. Begin with myself (not trying to change others).

2. Begin within myself (hence, without impetus from outside).

3. Open myself to the whole of reality (not a "specialized" spirituality).

4. Begin where I myself am: no *tabula rasa,* no waiting for the best, ideal point of departure. For example, "once I have money . . . ," "once I get married . . . ," "once I have managed to do this or that . . . ," "once I am a better person . . . !"

5. Do not consider the consequences. Here one needs a pure heart; otherwise one will be afraid. No one can calculate all consequences ahead of time, not even a computer; and once I put my trust in a computer, I am no longer free.

6. Be in solidarity—hence, not in isolation. Solitude need not mean isolation; solidarity can mean group, family, friends, whatever.

7. Be self-motivated—hence, without outside help, without financial support from outside, without predetermination, without a fixed goal. The true self can never be motivated by a goal!

8. Be nonviolent—not straining the will, not wanting to overcome anything. Otherwise one is merely repressing constantly.

9. Always make a fresh start!

You have said that christianity should break with the abrahamic traditions so that it can overcome the structure of a jewish sect. That sounds very pretentious. Could you explain that?

I would like to say, first of all, that judaism is, in my opinion, one of the greatest religious traditions of the world. I am simply against any kind of exclusivism. Until now, one had to be in a spiritual sense a semite, in an intellectual sense a greek, in order to become a christian. Otherwise one could not understand anything about christianity. For the first two millennia, christianity has identified with this position. That is magnificent—but is it enough?

Many great world traditions believed themselves either to be the only ones or to be superior to the others. A dramatic example of the first instance is the development of the scientific worldview; many religions are behaving in this same exclusivist and possessive manner. An example of the second instance would be the chinese, who are too smart to regard their tradition as the only one, but they consider themselves superior! They were the first to invent the word "barbarian" in order to belittle others.

By the expression "a second Council of Jerusalem" I mean the following: christianity could either limit itself to its existing former tradition—which would be totally legitimate. This would mean that christianity would be one religion beside others—no better, no worse—with all its differentiations and nuances. Or christianity could go through a mutation, could take a new step, equal to the step of the first christians at the first Council of Jerusalem, where they abolished circumcision. Thus, one would not only have to reinterpret baptism, among many other things, but also go beyond these christian concepts into the void opening up behind them. This is the challenge of the third millennium.

The word "christendom" means one thousand years of Europe in the political and cultural sense. The word "christianness," however, describes the development all the way up to the third millennium, where all doctrinal interpretations are neither omitted nor absolutized. Its main focus is on experience. Then one can be a christian for whom council-related systems of christian theology are no longer necessary—no matter how beautifully coined. We christians must determine collectively, as a church, what we want to be and to become. Both the traditional and the new forms are legitimate, but one must avoid one thing—perpetuating colonialism. If we were to choose the first form, it would mean ultimately that christianity could no longer be enculturated in Africa and Asia. After all, humanity cannot reduce itself to a single one of its branches. Along with Teilhard de Chardin one could show that even the concept of a monolithic human development is insufficient. I am talking about mutual fecundation.

What is it concretely that we have to overcome?

Only the claim to absoluteness and the claim to universality are to be overcome; nothing else stands in the way. One has to make room for other traditions, for the awareness that there are thought patterns with which the christian worldview does not know what to do. Up to now, one had to undergo a circumcision of the mind, of the intellect to be able to understand christianity. For the future, one may no longer require that.

Where do you see Man's chance for continued development? Christianity is quite captivated by moral teachings, and for the internal development of the human being very little is offered. Thus, the person always remains a sinner possibly able, through humility and repentance, to gain a place in heaven. But such a view does not exhaust the human potential! Rather, there should be a way and there is one—I feel—intended by God, whereby the person's destiny on earth is truly fulfilled and the person can develop a higher form of consciousness. This possibility is apparently not offered to us by christianity. I might only find it in Meister Eckhart's writings. Perhaps, one could go farther on this path, but it certainly is not the christian mainstream.

If this is the way you see christianity, you need to be converted—not in order to rescue some part of this kind of christianity but to rescue yourself and not remain stuck somewhere. If this is your idea of christianity, it is high time to liberate yourself from it toward a better kind of christianity, or toward something else.

My understanding of christianity differs from yours. In all religions, both institutionalized and noninstitutionalized, people are asking: "Where do I find a pure and proper sacred place for *me*? Must I cut my umbilical cord, discard my christianity, leave my hindu identity. . . ? Where can I find a religion suitable for me?" In this question, my own human weaknesses and those of other people come to the fore. Yet it makes little sense to console myself by uncovering mistakes in others, by regarding christianity as terrible, other people as naïve, and still others as fanatic.

One will have to take a step in the direction of love, tolerance, justice, and mainly freedom, if one wants to change anything here. There are certainly attractive ideas around; we may find them in

Aurobindo, in Meister Eckhart, and also in Pope John Paul II, but the difficulty is the practical application. If I were only tolerant of those who are tolerant themselves, my tolerance level would be very low.

But one should not be afraid. If you feel that christianity has been terrible for you, you should put it aside; there are other ways. I am quite serious about that. One needs to go one's own way existentially, and all paths lead to the goal, but only under one condition— that they are *paths;* that we do not become stuck but remain still on our way; and that we are not jumping from one path to the next in order to mix an individual cocktail. All paths are only then true paths when I *walk* them, walk on them and leave them behind. One tradition of medieval hinduism teaches the path of the paradox; it says that one can reach God even by hating God. That is also a path! One cannot say more, except: Be on your way!

Abbreviations

AV	*Atharva Veda*
BG	*Bhagavadgītā*
BU	*Brihadāranyaka Upanishad*
CU	*Chāndogya Upanishad*
DW	Meister Eckhart, *Die deutschen Werke* (Stuttgart: Kohlhammer, 1956ff.)
LW	Meister Eckhart, *Die Lateinischen Werke* (Stuttgart: Kohlhammer, 1956ff.)
MundU	*Mundaka Upanishad*
O.o.	Bonaventure, *Opera omnia,* ed. Quaracchi, 1892–1902
PG	*Patrologia Cursus Completus: Series Graeca,* ed. J.-P. Migne (Paris, 1857–1866)
PL	*Series Latina*
SB	Shatapatha Brāhmana
Sent.	Bonaventure, *Commentaria in Quator Libros Sententiarum Magistri Petri Lombardi,* O.o., vols. I–IV

Books of the Bible are abbreviated in standard form.

Notes

Chapter 1

1. The Wisdom of Solomon and its predecessors, for example, the work of the Egyptian Amenope (who lived at least one thousand years earlier), could be viewed as sacral forms of this prudence. Yahweh says to Job that "to fear the Lord is wisdom and to avoid evil is prudence" (Job XXVIII: 28), which correlates with Prov. I:7.

2. They have been newly documented in Thomas Schipflinger, *Sophia—Maria* (Munich and Zürich: Verlag Neue Stadt, 1988).

3. For a good introduction to the old problem, see the essays on *sophia* in *Theologisches Wörterbuch zum Neuen Testament,* ed. G. Kittel and G. Friedrich (Stuttgart: Kohlhammer); for the Hebrew Bible, compare the essays in *Theologisches Wörterbuch zum Alten Testament,* ed. G. Botterweck and H. Ringgren (Stuttgart: Kohlhammer).

4. Job XXVIII:28; see also n. 1. The Vulgate translates: "*Ecce timor ipsa Domini est sapientia, et recedere a malo intelligentia.*" Augustine (*De Trinitate 14.1*) *distinguishes between* eusebeia *and* theosebeia, *summarizing both concepts as* "*Dei cultus.*" He translates: "*Ecce pietas est sapientia; abstinere autem a malis, scientia.*" Concerning Bonaventure, compare *Sententiarium* III, d.35,a.u.,q.1 (*Opera omnia,* ed. Quaracchi, III: 774).

5. Heraclitus, fragment 112. "Thinking in a healthy fashion is the greatest perfection, and wisdom consists in speaking the truth and acting according to nature by listening to the latter."

6. Heraclitus, fragment 41. Diels translates: "Only one thing is wise, understanding the thought, which knows how to steer everything in its own way."

7. See my book *The Silence of God* (Maryknoll, N.Y.: Orbis Books, 1989).

8. As, for example, Abhinavagupta, *Parâtrîshikâ-vivarana,* passim.

9. Heraclitus, fragment 40: "Knowing it all [*polymathia*] does not teach reason [*nous*]" (Diels). In another place, Diels translates *nous* as "mental force" (*Paideia,* 242).

10. Fumi Sakaguchi writes that "Buddhism, consequently, discards the thought method of differentiations and opposites, the analytical way of thinking" (*Der Begriff der Weisheit in den Hauptwerken Bonaventuras* [Munich and Salzburg: Pustet, 1968], p.77).

11. Dionysius Areopagita, *De mystica Theologia* I,3 (*PG* 3:1001).

12. Thomas Aquinas, *Summa Theologiae* I,q.12,a.13,ad 1.

13. *Illud est ultimum cognitionis humanae de Deo quod sciat se Deum nescire in quantum cognoscit illud quod Deus est* (*De potentia* VII,5,ad 14).

14. Evagrius Ponticus, *Kephalaia Gnostica, Centuria* III, 88.

15. BU II,4,14: "That by which everything is understood, how can one understand it? How can one understand that which understands?" (*yenaidam sarvam vijânâti, tam kena vijânîyât, vijñâtâram are kena vijânîyât*).

16. See my essay "Die existentielle Phänomenologie der Wahrheit" *Philosophisches Jahrbuch der Görresgesellschaft* 64 (1956), 27–54.

17. Cited by V. Böhtlingk, *Indische Sprüche* (St. Petersburg, 1870–1873; Weisbaden: Harrassowitz, 1966), Saying 6741.

18. *"Ab intellectu inchoandum est, et perveniendum ad sapientiam"* (Bonaventure, *Hexaemeron,* col. 3, n.1 [O.o. V, 343a]).

19. *Avijñātam vijānatām vijñātam avijānatām;* cf. also *Rig Veda* I,164,32.

20. See I Cor. I:19–23, 26–30; II:4–7; III:18–20; IV:10; Col. II:8; Rom. XII:2; etc.

21. See my essay "La dialéctica de la razón armada," *Concordia* 9 (1986), 68–89.

22. *"Haec igitur sapientia dicitur multiformis, quia multi sunt modi exprimendi, . . . ut etiam veletur superbis, aperiatur humilibus"* (Bonaventure, *Hexaemeron,* col.2, n.12 [O.o. V, 338b]). The biblical connotations are here apparent: cf. Luke I:51–53; 10:21; Matt. XI:25; etc.

23. See Meister Eckhart, *Von Abgeschiedenheit, Deutsche Werke,* vol. 5, ed. J. Quint (Stuttgart: Kohlhammer, 1963), pp. 377–458 (text, pp. 400–437; translation, pp. 539–547).

24. *"Neque enim propter stellas homo, sed stellae propter hominem factae sunt,"* (Gregory the Great, *Homilia X in Evang.,* on Matt. II:1–12).

25. *Sapiens homo dominatur et astris* (Thomas Aquinas, *Summa Theologiae* I, q.115,a.4,ad 3; cf. also I–II,q.77,a.1).

26. This is emphasized, and justly so, by M. Machovec, *Die Rückkehr zur Weisheit: Philosophie angesichts des Abgrundes* (Stuttgart: Kreuz, 1988), pp. 87ff.

27. *"Etad guhyam mahāguhyam"* in *Paratrīshikā* 2, by Abhinavagupta, *Paratrīshikā-vivarana,* trans. J. Singh, ed. B. Bäumer (Delhi, 1988), p. 18; cf. also pp. 53ff. The word is translated by Abhinavagupta either as "this secret, big secret" or as "this secret, a non-secret." The stem *guh* means literally "concealing," "covering," "keeping secret"; *guha* means "hidden

space," "cave," "ditch"; *guhya* is understood as hidden space and as a symbol for something secret (cf. also BG IX,1–2, where it talks about *guhyātamam* and *rājaguhyam*).

28. See n. 20 above.

29. There is a play here on the words *oikia* and *monê:* one house, many dwellings, many homesteads.

30. *"Mens nostra . . . a divina sapientia tamquam domus Dei inhabitur"* (Bonaventure, *Itinerarium mentis in Deum* IV,8 [O.o. V, 308]). For Bonaventure it is clear that "in any thing perceived or known, God hides within" (*in omni re, quae sentitur sive quae cognoscitur, interius lateat ipse Deus*) (*De reductione artium ad theologiam* 26 [O.o. V, 325]).

31. See *Die Lehre von Amenenope* III,9–18. The entire chapter says that one should preserve and digest wisdom in the heart; cf. also A. Marzal, *La enseñanza de Amenenope* (Madrid: Marova, 1965), pp. 85ff.

32. BU III,9,23: *"Hridayena hi satyam jānāti—hridaye hy eva satyam pratishthitam bhavati—iti."* I have already said that *satyam* is the unfolding state of being being (*sat*), hence truth and wisdom.

33. *"Domus dei totus est mundus, domus dei ecclesia catholica est, domus dei etiam est quaelibet, fidelis anima"* (Hugh of St. Victor, *De arca Noe morali* I,1 [PL 176:721A]).

34. See Böhtlingk, *Indische Sprüche,* Saying 6074.

35. See Fung Yu-lan, *A History of Chinese Philosophy* (Princeton, N.J.: Princeton University Press, 1953), vol. 2 (1973), pp. 386–408, for the buddhist background of this otherwise taoist mentality.

36. This dialogue took place in St. Ursula's Church, Munich.

Chapter 2

1. See R. Panikkar, "Der Mensch—ein trinitarisches Mysterium" ("The person: A Trinitarian Mystery"), in *Die Verantwortung des Menschen für eine bewohnbare Welt im Christentum, Hinduismus und Buddhismus,* ed. R. Panikkar and W. Strolz (Freiburg: Herder, 1985), pp. 147–190.

2. Meister Eckhart, *Die Lateinischen Werke: Sermones,* ed. Joseph Koch et al. (Stuttgart: Kohlhammer, 1956).

3. F. Schelling, *Werke* (Stuttgart: Augsburg, 1856ff.), II,1,338.

4. This expression does not appear literally in either Ignatius's *Exercises* or in the *Constitutions,* although the adjective "indifferent" appears twice in the former and eight times in the latter. However, Ignatius's later years and the original spirituality of the Jesuits in general are filled with this "indifference."

5. Richard Wilhelm translates, "The one who is chosen is simplistic and bland."

6. Bonaventure, *Sententiarum* II,d.23,a.2,q.2 (O.o. [Ouaracchi] II, 49b): *"omne enim quod cognoscitur, cognoscitur per aliquid praesens."*

7. Cf. F. Ebner, *Fragmente, Aufsätze, Aphorismen* (Munich: Kösel, 1963), especially Fragment 2 (Einsamkeit: Ich und Du), pp. 87–95, and "Die Entdeckung das Ich und Du," pp. 800–819; M. Buber, *Das Dialogische Prienzip* (Heidelburg: L. Schneider), 1962, especially "Ich und Du," pp. 7–136.

8. R. Wilhelm translates, "Without this something, there is no I."

9. Bonaventure, *Hexaemeron,* col. 2, n. 32 (O.o. V): *"dicitur tenebrae, quia intellectus non capit."*

10. Ibid., col. 13, n. 12 (O.o. V, 390a): *"Iste liber, scilicet mundus, quasi emortuus et deletus erat."*

11. Bonaventure, *Breviloquium,* q.2, c.12 (O.o. V, 230a).

12. Bonaventure, *Sententiarum* III,d.23,a.1,q.4,ad 5 (O.o. III, 482): *"Ad illud quod obiicitur, quod quanto scientia nobilior est, tanto certior, dicendum quod illud non habet veritatem."*

13. Dionysius, *Epist.* I (*Caio monacho*), PG 3:1065a. The traditional translation says: *"Et si quis, viso Deo, cognovit id quod vidit, nequaquam ipsum vidit."*

14. See chapter 1, n. 27.

15. See p. 18.

16. *Pantôn de malista aischuneo sauton.* One could also translate this as "honor thyself," if honor, like *aischunê,* conveys both modesty (shame) and honor. See above.

17. See R. Panikkar, *El concepto de naturaleza,* 2nd ed. (Madrid: C.S.I.C., 1972), esp. pp. 197–232.

18. Thomas Aquinas, *Summa Theologiae* I,q.34,a.3; see also I,q.37,a.2,ad 3, which says, *"Sicut Pater dicit se et omnem creaturam Verbo quod genuit, . . . ita diligit se et omnem creaturam Spiritus Sancto."*

Chapter 3

1. This motto is an allusion to Stefan George, "No thing be where the word breaks"; see also the commentary by Heidegger, "Das Wesen der Sprache" in *Unterwegs zur Sprache,* 5th ed. (Pfullingen: Neske, 1975), pp. 159ff. Of course, see also John I:14 ("And the Word became flesh") and the well-known poem by John of the Cross.

2. The author is playing here with the common etymology of the words "meditation," "medicine," and "moderation."

3. Regarding the motto of this chapter: S. George has written: "Kein Ding sei wo das Wort gebricht." The poem entitled *Das Wort (The Word)* was first published in 1919 and reprinted in his book of poems *Das Neue Reich.*

4. The author is playing a word game here of "ultimate concern" (Paul Tillich) and "ultimate unconcern"; religion as freedom, liberation.

5. L. Massignon, *La passion de Husayn Ibn Mansûr Hallâj* (Paris: Guenther, 1922; reprint, 1975), vol. 3, pp. 300ff.

6. Thomas Aquinas, *Summa Theologiae* II,q.1,a.1: "*actus autem credentis non terminatur ad enuntiabile, sed ad rem.*"

Chapter 4

1. My publications concerning this subject matter include "*Sobre el sentido cristiano de la vida*" in *Arbor,* no. 64 (Madrid, 1951), also published in my book *Humanismo y Cruz* (Madrid: Rialp, 1963), pp. 112–177; and "*Què vol dir avui confessar-se cristià,*" in *Questions de vida cristiana* no. 128/29 (Monserrat: Publicacions de l'Abadia de Montserrat, 1985), pp. 86–111.

2. I would like to emphasize that, although I have written extensively on these subjects, practice (in form of dialogues, get-togethers, projects, activities) has always been right by my side. In fact, that which I have said and done in practice may be more important than what I have written and published.

3. This essay should be understood in light of some of my former publications, for example: *Die vielen Götter und der eine Herr: Beiträge zum ökonomischen Gespräch der Weltreligionen.* (Weilheim: O. W. Barth, 1963); *The Unknown Christ of Hinduism* (Maryknoll, N.Y.: Orbis Books, 1980), *Religionen und die Religion* (Munich: Hueber, 1965), "Salvation in Christ: Concreteness and Universality, the Supername," opening lecture at the Ecumenical Institute of Advanced Theological Studies (Jerusalem: Tantur, 1972). A shorter version of the first part is published, titled "The Meaning of Christ's Name in the Universal Economy of Salvation," in *Evangelization, Dialogue and Development,* ed. M. Dhavamony (Rome, 1972), pp. 195–218; trans. *The Intrareligious Dialogue* (1978); "Ritatatva: A Preface to a Hindu-Christian Theology," *Jeevadhara* 49 (1979), 6–63.

4. We should not forget that the expression "Body of Christ" denotes, according to tradition, first the christian people and only later the Eucharist. See here F. Holböck, *Der eucharistische und der mystische Leib Christi* (Rome, 1941); and H. de Lubac, *Corpus mysticum* (Paris, 1949); also idem, *Méditation sur l'Eglise* (Paris: Aubier, 1954).

5. See, e.g., Hajime Nakamura, *Ways of Thinking of Eastern People* (Honolulu: University of Hawaii Press, 1985).

6. See my essay "Religion and Politics: The Western Dilemma," in *Religion and Politics in the Modern World,* ed. P. H. Merkl and N. Smart (New York: New York University Press, 1985), pp. 44–60. Mahâtmâ Gandhi is believed to have said without hesitation, yet full of humility, that "those saying religion has nothing to do with politics do not know what religion is" (*An Autobiography of the Story of My Experiments with Truth,* trans. M. Desai [Ahmedabad: Navajivan, 1982], p. 420).

7. See my book *Kultmysterium im Hinduismus und Christentum: Ein Beitrag zur vergleichenden Religionstheologie* (Freiburg and Munich: Alber, 1964), French trans. *Le mystère du culte dans l'hinouisme et le christianisme* (Paris: Cerf, 1970), pp. 37ff.

8. The last stanza of the *Rig Veda* (X,191,4) is a song in praise of religious harmony.

9. See Part III of this book; for more detail, see my "The Invisible Harmony: A Universal Theory of Religion or a Cosmic Confidence in Reality?" in *Toward a Universal Theology of Religion,* ed. Leonard Swidler (Maryknoll, N.Y.: Orbis Books, 1987).

10. The word "christic," rather than "christian," is used in connection with the word principle; it is to denote the basic characteristic of the christian faith.

11. See my chapter "Christianity and World Religions" in *Christianity* (Patiala: Punjabi University, 1969), pp. 78–127, Guru Nanak Quincentennial Collection Series, where these five epochs are discussed in greater detail; revised edition "Autoconciencia cristiana y religiones" in *Fe cristiana y sociedad moderna* (Madrid: Ediciones sm, 1989), vol. 26, pp. 199–267.

12. Paul Knitter's book was respectively titled *No Other Name? A Critical Survey of Christian Attitudes Toward the World Religions,* American Society of Missiology Series, 7 (Maryknoll, N.Y.: Orbis Books, 1985). In the preface to this series, W. J. Danker, president of the editors circle, wrote: "At the center of attention will always be Christian mission." And he specifies: "By 'mission' is meant here a crossing over into other cultures, across the borders of faith in Jesus Christ and its absence" (p. XI). The collection of essays resulting from the 1981 SEDOS seminar in Rome concerning "the future of mission"—102 people from 45 Catholic religious communities and six continents attended—received the title *Mission in Dialogue,* ed. M. Motte and J. R. Lang (Maryknoll, N.Y.: Orbis Books, 1982).

13. See my essay "Dialogical Dialogue" in *The World's Religious Traditions,* Festschrift Wilfred Cantwell Smith, ed. Frank Whaling (Edinburgh: T. & T. Clark, 1984), pp. 61–72; see also my "Begegnung der Religionen," in *Dialog der Religionen* I,1 (1991), pp. 9–39.

14. In a yet unpublished thesis paper, titled "Das Heil der Welt" (the salvation of the world), I have tried to demonstrate in what way this idea is common to salvation-oriented religions. It is ultimately the subconscious transposition of a natural law: one out of millions of human semen becomes a human being; one of millions of living species becomes the human species; one of millions of plants becomes an animal, and so forth. One says, respectively, that only few peoples in the world are christian, and even fewer are divinized, saved, realized.

15. I would like to point out that the ambiguous title of one of my first books on this subject, *The Unknown Christ of Hinduism,* does not refer to

the Christ known to Christians and unknown to Hindus, but to *the unknown Christ in Hinduism*—and even more so in christianity. See note 4. Also see K. Healy, *Christ as Common Ground: A Study of Christianity and Hinduism* (Pittsburgh: Duquesne University Press, 1990).

16. For a representative voice on the present North American debate, see Wilfred Cantwell Smith, *Toward a World Theology* (Philadelphia: Westminster Press, 1981).

17. The title of an otherwise excellent book by Karl Prümm shows what I am trying to say: *Christentum als Neuheitserlebnis* [Christianity, the new experience] (Freiburg, Herder, 1939).

18. See R. Panikkar, "Religious Pluralism: The Metaphysical Challenge," in *Religious Pluralism,* ed. Leroy S. Rouner (Notre Dame, Ind.: University of Notre Dame Press, 1984), pp. 97–115.

19. R. Panikkar, "Aporias in the Comparative Philosophy of Religion," *Man and World* 13 (1980), pp. 357–383; see also my "What is Comparative Philosophy Comparing?" in *Interpreting Across Boundaries,* ed. G. I. Larson and E. Deutsch (Princeton, N.J.: Princeton University Press, 1988), pp. 116–136.

20. See my essay "The Dream of an Indian Ecclesiology," in *In Search of an Indian Ecclesiology* (Bangalore: Indian Theological Association, 1985), pp. 25–54.

21. See n. 11 above.

22. K. Rahner and J. Ratzinger say: "It is known . . . , that the New Testament nowhere understands itself as 'Scripture'; for the former, 'Scripture' is only the Old Testament, while the Christ message [Gospel] is simply 'spirit', which teaches understanding it [the Old Testament]" (*Episkopat und Primat* [Freiburg: Herder, 1961], p. 47).

23. However, it is certain that many former or "fallen Christians," who came during the sixties and seventies to Varanasi at the Ganges as "converted" Hindus, attained after their return home in the eighties a new Christian identity.

24. See n. 9 above.

25. See my essay "L'eau et la mort: Réflection interculturelle sur une métaphore," in *Filosofia e religione di fronte all morte,* ed. M. Olivetti (Padoua: CEDAM, 1981), pp. 481–502.

26. See my essay "Singularity and Individuality: The Double Principle of Individuation," in *Revue Internationale de Philosophie,* Festschrift Raymond Klibansky, no. 111/12 (1975), 141–165.

27. See my essay "Salvation in Christ" as n. 3 above.

28. See my essay "Colligite Fragmenta: For an Integration of Reality," in *From Alienation to At-One-ness,* ed. F. A. Eigo and S. E. Fittipaldi (Villanova, Penn.: The Villanova University Press, 1977), pp. 19–91. See also n. 1 of chapter 2 and my recent book *The Cosmotheandric Experience* (Maryknoll, N.Y.: Orbis Books, 1993).

29. See my essay "Le concept d'ontonomie," for the XI. International Congress on Philosophy, Brussels, Louvrain: Nauwelaerts, 1953), vol. 3, pp. 182ff.

30. See my *Ontonomía de la ciencia: Sobre el sentido de la Ciencia y sus relaciones con la Filosofia* (Madrid, Gredos, 1961).

31. One could mention such names as I. Barbour, D. Bohm, F. Capra, K. Pribram, I. Prigogine, R. Sheldrake, and their predecessors B. Bavink, P. Duhem, A. Koyré, and many others.

32. As examples, one might mention: *Cosmogony and Ethical Order,* ed. R. W. Lovin and F. E. Reynolds (Chicago: University of Chicago Press, 1985); S. H. Nasr, "The Role of the Traditional Sciences in the Encounter of Religion and Science—An Oriental Perspective" *Religious Studies* 20/4 (1984), 519–541; see also his earlier book *An Introduction to Islamic Cosmological Doctrines* (Cambridge, Mass., 1964; rev. ed. 1978). Useful also is W. F. Warren, *The Earliest Cosmologies* (New York: Earon & Mains, 1909), as a historical document for the early modern interest; also the remarkable essay by S. Toulmin, *The Return of Cosmology* (Berkeley: University of California Press, 1982).

33. See J. S. O'Leary, *Questioning Back: The Overcoming of Metaphysics in Christian Tradition* (Oak Grove, Minn.: Winston-Seabury Press, 1985); also, "Overcoming the Nicean Creed," *Cross Currents* 34/4 (Winter 1984), 405–413.

34. See my first essay on this problem, "La demitologizzazione nell'incontro tra cristianesimo e induismo," in *Il problema della demitizzazione,* ed. E. Castelli (Padua: CEDAM, 1961), pp. 243–266.

35. For the interaction between *mythos* and *logos* in each of the conceptions of the world, see *Ancient Cosmologies,* ed. C. Blacker (London, 1975).

36. See my essay "The Myth of Pluralism: The Tower of Babel—A meditation on Non-Violence," *Cross Currents* 29/2 (1979), 197–230.

37. See my essay "La religión del futuro—o la crisis del concepto de religión: La religiosidad humana," in *Civiltà delle machine* (Rome) 27 (1979), 82–91; here the first of twelve points says: "The problem of the future of religion is not that of the religion of the future"; and the eleventh says: "The future of religion is, first of all, a personal religiousness and not a singular religious confession."

Glossary

actio (lat.):   activity, doing

adhidaivika (skr.):   spiritual, belonging to the divine

advaita, advaitic (skr.):   "nondualist, nondualism"; the teaching that the absolute is without a second. God and the World are neither one nor two. So are *âtman* and *brahman*.

agapê (greek):   "love"

agni (skr.):   "fire"; Vedic deity of fire

aham (skr.):   "I"

aiôn (greek):   the world's time, eternity; also, age.

aisthêsis (greek):   sense perception, sensation, sense, aesthetics

ākāsha (skr.):   "(empty) space"; in Hinduism, the last of the five elements (earth, water, fire, air, and space or ether)

ānanda (skr.):   bliss; along with *sat* and *cit,* the three dimensions of *brahman* or the absolute reality

anātman, anātmavāda, nairātmyavāda (skr.):   the teaching that things are without a fixed, substantial characteristic center. There is no *âtman,* no fixed substance.

anātmavādin (skr.):   a follower of the *anâtman* doctrine

anima naturaliter Christiana (lat.):   "the soul is christian by nature"

artha (skr.):   wealth, riches. One of the four *purushārthas* or goals of life.

ātman (skr.):   "self"; the core of Man, which does not perish

ātmavāda (skr.):   doctrine of *ātman* as the eternal characteristic of Man

ātmavādin (skr.):   a follower of the *ātman* doctrine

avatāra (skr.):   "the coming down" (of a God to earth in human or animal form)

Bhagavadgītā (skr.):   "song of the Lord"; famous Indic doctrinal poem in the *Mahābhārata,* often called the "New Testament of hinduism"

bhakti (skr.):   love, devotion to God; one of the indic paths to salvation by means of union with the deity

brahman (skr.):   soul of the world, the world's essence; the One, penetrating and uniting within itself everything; the absolute

bodhisattva (skr.):   enlightened being in the māhāyana tradition; the blessed soul who renounces *nirvāna* for the sake of helping all other sentient beings to their enlightenment

chronocentrism: placing today's time and one's respective spirit of the times (*Zeitgeist*) first when interpretating the world; from the greek *chronos* ("time") and latin *centrum* ("center, middle"); see also *ethnocentrism*

circulus vitiosus (lat.): "vicious circle"; faulty logic, which already pre-supposes what is to be proved

cit (skr.): consciousness, intellect

civitas Dei and civitas terrena (lat.): "city of God" and "earthly city"; Augustine's (354–430) teaching of two "cities"

coincidentia oppositorum (lat.): the coming together of opposites

Conquista (span.): spanish crusades in the Americas after 1492, especially the conquest of Mexico (1519–1521) and of Peru (1532–1533)

contemplatio (lat.): considering the world as God's temple, and thus a holistic union of reality, including our action in it

cosmotheandric: "World-God-Man related"; from Greek *kosmos, theos,* and *anêr.* See Theanthropocosmic.

creatio continua (lat.): "continued creation"; doctrine of the continued creative activity of God in terms of constantly creating the world

deus ex machina (lat.): "God from a machine"; term from classic tragedy: at the end of the play, a God is rolled on stage so that the unsolvable is finally solved

Dhammapada (pāli): buddhist collection of sayings of the Pâli Canon

dharma (skr.): central notion of indic philosophy with various meanings: eternal, fixed order of the world, lawfulness, harmony, doctrine, normative basis of actions, morality, custom, rite, law, "religion"

dharmakāya (skr.): "body of *dharma*"; in mahāyāna buddhism, the basic characteristic of the Buddha, which is, simultaneously, the basic characteristic of the world's beings, the essence of reality

dharmakshetra (skr.): the field of *dharma*

diachronic (greek): extending through time

diatopic (greek): extending through space

doxa (greek): splendor, superiority, magnificence, opinion

dualism: view of a basic division of being into two mutually irreducible principles, especially spirit and matter, soul and body

epistêmê (greek): science, scientific knowledge

epochê (greek): "holding in"; placing subjective value judgments in parentheses when describing phenomena *eros* (greek):   love, lust, and sensual love

ethnocentrism: making one's own people's culture the measuring rod for judging other cultures; from greek *ethnos* ("people") and latin *centrum* ("center")

eusebeia (greek):   piety, religion, love and respect for the Gods

exclusivism, inclusivism, pluralism: terms for an attitude toward non-christian religions: exclusivism regards the latter as not leading to salvation; inclusivism absolutizes salvation in Christ on the one hand yet on the other offers other religions a place in it; pluralism acknowledges the mutual irreducibility of worldviews

fides quaerens intellectum (lat.):   "faith seeking understanding" (Anselm of Canterbury, 1033–1109); important theological program of the Middle Ages

ghat: stairway along the banks of the Ganges and other rivers

hermeneutics, hermeneutic (from greek):   "the art of interpretation"; theory and method of understanding and interpreting of texts

homeomorphic: "of similar form"; that means, of comparable importance and function in the context of another religious or cultural system; from greek *homoios* ("similar") and *morphē* ("form"). Analogy of a third degree.

humanum (lat.):   the basic human trait; that specific to humanity

inclusivism: see *exclusivism*

Ishvara (skr.):   "lord of the universe"; personal god, in contrast to the impersonal *brahman*

jīva (skr.):   soul or life, the embodied *ātman*

jñāna (skr.):   "higher knowledge, understanding"; one of the paths to salvation

kairos, kairological (greek):   a special time, a nonquantitative perception of time

kāma (skr.):   desire, passion, sensual lust, love

karma, karman (skr.):   deed, work, doing, which falls back to the one performing it and adheres to him or her

kat' holon (greek):   all-embracing, as a whole

kosmos (greek):   order, the ordered world, the entirety of the world

kurukshetra (skr.):   the field of the Kauravas where the battle of the Māhābhārata took place. In connection with the *dharmakshetra* it represents the theandric battle of life.

li (chin.):   "rites," "morality" in the confucian tradition, order *logos* (greek):   word, thought, judgment, reason. In the New Testament, Christ as the Word of God (John I)

Mahābhārata: Indian epic of the struggle between the Pandavas and the Kauravas

Mahāyāna Buddhism: "big vehicle of transportation"; school of Buddhism that originated in India after theranāda buddhism.

manas (skr.):   mind, reason, ability to perceive and think

metanoia (greek):   change of mind, conversion, overcoming of mind (Matt. I:14)

metron (greek):   measure, measuring rod

moksha (skr.):   liberation, ultimate goal, salvation; homeomorphic to *sôtêria*

monism (from the Greek *monos,* singular):   reducing all things to the singular principle, active in them

morphê (greek):   form, appearance, essence

morphology (from greek):   doctrine about form, especially about the developmental stages of all living things and of culture

mythos (greek):   "word," "narrative"; already in antiquity distinguished from *logos;* a requirement for the *logos*'s existence; horizon of intelligibility.

nairātmyavāda (skr.):   see *anātmavāda*

nāma-rūpa (skr.):   name and form, the world of appearances

neti–neti (skr.):   "not that . . . , not that"; denotes the unpronounceability of what truly is

Nicene Creed: the most important of ecclesiological creeds, originally formulated in 325 at the Council of Nicaea: expanded in 381 in the Council of Constantinople

nirguna brahma (skr.):   *brahman* without characteristics, the One being without any other

nirvāna (skr.):   term for salvation; probably meaning "ceasing to burn"

nixus, nisus (lat.):   élan, energy

noêma (from greek):   in the phenomenology of E. Husserl, the unity of intellectual perception; see *phenomenology*

noetics, noetic: doctrine on thought, understanding

nomos (greek):   custom, rule, law

Nostra aetate: the "Declaration concerning the relationship of the Church to non-Christian religions" of the Second Vatican Council (1962–1965) *ontonomy, ontonomic:* internal order of being, whereby the concrete individual is both independent from and integrated in the totality of being. Neither the severed independence of each individual (autonomy) nor a hierarchy of individuals (heteronomy) but rather the interrelatedness of being is viewed as the point of departure for thought (from the greek *on* ("being") and *nomos* ("law," "order")

orthodoxy, orthopraxy (from greek):   "proper doctrine"; "proper acting"

pars pro toto (lat.):   the part standing for the whole

perichôrêsis (greek) and *circumincessio* (lat.):   terms of the christian doctrine on the trinity, describing the mutual interpenetration of the divine persons, the Father, the Son, and the Holy Spirit

phenomenology (from greek *phainomai,* "to appear"):   teaching about appearances; philosophical school founded by Edmund Husserl (1859–1938); also, a school in the study of comparative religion, which asks about the nature of religion and the religious as it presents itself in its various "forms of appearance"

physis (greek):   nature

pisteuma: parallel to *noêma* and deduced from the greek *pisteuô,* "believe": the intended meaning of religious phenomena

pluralism: see *exclusivism*

polis (greek):   the city-state of Greek antiquity

pratītyasamutpāda (skr.):   Buddhist teaching on the "conditional development" or "development in dependence," meaning that nothing is through its own doing and carries the conditions for its existence within; instead, everything is dependent on something else in the cycle of existence

prema (skr.):   love, love of God

purusha (skr.):   Man, primordial Man, Adam

psychê (greek):   soul, disposition, heart, enlivened being

quaternitas perfecta (lat.):   the perfected fourfoldness

Râmâyana: indic heroic epic

ratio (lat.):   reason, thinking

saeculum (lat.):   the age of the world, age, century, the world

secular: on this side, in these times, in the world (from Latin *saeculum*)

saguna brahman (skr.):   "*brahman* with characteristics" in symbolic form

sangha (skr. or pāli):   the buddhist community; in a stricter sense, the order of nuns and monks *sat* (skr.):   being; homeomorphic to the latin *esse*

satori (jap.):   experience of enlightenment in zen

Septuagint (lat.):   "the seventy" (translators), jewish translation of the Hebrew Bible into greek, made from the third to the first century B.C. in Alexandria

Shiva, Shivaism, Shivaitic: one of the major deities of India; one of the two major religions of hinduism

shraddhā (skr.):   belief, trust (in the teachings of the Veda or in God)

shūnyatā (skr.):   emptiness, void; a central teaching of mahâyâna buddhism

sôma (greek):   body

sophia (greek):   wisdom

sotêria (greek):   salvation, wholeness, liberation

sui generis (lat.):   "in its own way"

sushupti (skr.):   deep, dreamless sleep; one of four states of consciousness (*avasthā*) apart from waking, dreaming, and the transconscious state of enlightenment

svadharma (skr.):   the individual manifestation of a *dharma* in every person

svayamprakāsha (skr.):   "self-enlightening," self-refulgent

tao (chin.):   "path"; central notion of Chinese philosophy, especially of Taoism, way, ultimate

Tao-te ching (*Tao-te king*) (chin.):   "the book of the path and its power"; main work of philosophical Taoism in China, attributed to Lao-tzu (sixth century B.C.); historically proved to have existed at least since the third century B.C.

tat tvam asi (skr.):   "this is you"; statement in the *Upanishads* that *âtman* is ultimately *brahman*

technê (greek):   art, dexterity, craft

theandric: "god-human" (from greek *theos* and *anēr*)

theanthropocosmic: "God-Human-World-related" (from greek *theos, anthrôpos,* and *kosmos*). See cosmotheandric.

theosebeia (greek):   religious adoration, cult of the divine

topos/topoi (greek):   place, spot

triloka (skr.):   "three-world-related"; in Hinduism denoting heaven, earth, underworld

trisangam (skr.):   the coming together of three rivers. The term *sanga* means uniting/flowing together of two rivers. The term *trisangam* points to the *sanga* of the Ganges and Jamunâ, as well as of the invisible subterranean Sarasvatî in Allahabad

upadesha (skr.): instruction of a master

Upanishads (skr.): indic philosophical texts, described as "the epitome of the Veda"

Veda (skr.): "knowledge"; oldest sacred text of India of nonhuman origin and particular authority

vedânta (skr.): end of the Vedas or one of the latest philosophical schools of hindu thought, Shankara and Râmânuja being among the most famous representatives.

vedantin: an adherent to Vedânta

vidyā (skr.): "knowledge," "understanding"

wu-wei (chin.): "not-doing" in Taoist philosophy

yoga (skr.): "yoke"; path to enlightenment and union with the divine

Sources

Chapter I

—"Preparing a Dwelling Place for Wisdom": Lecture with ensuing discussion, St. Ursula church, Munich, March 14, 1990 (first publication); formulation of theme by Irmgard Hafner, Munich.

Chapter II

—"*Quaternitas Perfecta*": Lectures and discussions at a retreat conference at the retreat center Domicilium, Weyarn/Upper Bavaria, March 16–18, 1990 (first publication).

Chapter III

—"Philosophy as Life-style": Expanded edition of the essay "Philosophy as Lifestyle/Philosophie als Lebensstil" in *Philosophes critiques d'eux-memes,* ed. A. Mercier and M. Svilar, vol. IV (Berne, 1978), vol. 4, pp. 209–220; 209–220; translated from the German text.

—"Questions and Answers on Life-style": see Part II.

Chapter IV

—"Trisangam": Expanded edition of the essay "The Jordan, the Tiber, and the Ganges: Three Kairological Moments of Christic Self-Consciousness," in *The Myth of Christian Uniqueness: Toward a Pluralistic Theology of Religions,* ed. John Hick and Paul. F. Knitter (Maryknoll, N.Y.: Orbis Books, 1987), pp. 89–116; translated from the German text.

—"This Is You: Questions and Answers in Summary": Concluding discussion at the retreat center Domicilium, March 18, 1990; see above.